Black Voluntary and Community Sector funding

Black Voluntary and Community Sector funding

Its impact on civic engagement and capacity building

Karen Chouhan and Clarence Lusane

The **Joseph Rowntree Foundation** has supported this project as part of its programme of research and innovative development projects, which it hopes will be of value to policy makers, practitioners and service users. The facts presented and views expressed in this report are, however, those of the authors and not necessarily those of the Foundation.

Joseph Rowntree Foundation, The Homestead, 40 Water End, York YO30 6WP
Website: www. jrf.org.uk

Supported by the REDRAP Partnership.
(Race and Ethnic Diversity Research and Policy Partnership)
The REDRAP Partnership is a research consortium between The 1990 Trust, other Non-Government Organisations (NGOs) and academic institutions. De Montfort University, Leicester, were our main partners for this research.

A CIP catalogue record for this report is available from the British Library.

ISBN 1 85935 170 0   (paperback)
ISBN 1 85935 171 9   (pdf: available at www.jrf.org.uk)

Cover design by Adkins Design

Prepared and printed by:
York Publishing Services Ltd
64 Hallfield Road
Layerthorpe
York YO31 7ZQ
Tel: 01904 430033; Fax: 01904 430868; Website: www.yps-publishing.co.uk

Further copies of this report, or any other JRF publication, can be obtained either from the JRF website (www.jrf.org.uk/bookshop/) or from our distributor, York Publishing Services Ltd, at the above address.

Contents

Acknowledgements

- *1990 Trust Staff*: Audrey Adams, Cheryl Sealey, Haven Lutaaya, Lydia Brathwaite.

- *Steering group members*: Joe Allen (Chair, East Midlands Community Fund), Lee Jasper (Senior Policy Advisor to the Mayor of London on Policing and Equalities), Prof. Mark Johnson (De Montfort University), Rita Patel (Director, Belgrave Baheno Peepul Centre, Leicester), Prof. Richard Tomlins (De Montfort University), Dr Brian Williams (De Montfort University), Simon Woolley (Director, Operation Black Vote).

- *Community facilitators*: Ballu Patel and Naina Patel (Leicester); David James, Lloyd Johnson, Dipen Rajyaguru (London).

- *Focus group participants*: see Appendices for details.

- *Questionnaire respondents*: see Appendices for details.

- *Joseph Rowntree Foundation*.

- *Administrative support*: Fiona Hall of the Race and Ethnic Diversity Research and Policy Partnership (REDRAPP).

Glossary of terms

BME	Black and Minority Ethnic
BMEO	Black and Minority Ethnic Organisations
BVCS	Black Voluntary and Community Sector
CPFTL	City Parochial Foundation and Trust for London
CRE	Commission for Racial Equality
LDA	London Development Agency
LFEPA	London Fire and Emergency Planning Authority
LSP	Local Strategic Plan
NCADC	National Coalition of Anti-Deportation Campaigns
NCVO	National Council for Voluntary Organisations
NGO	Non-Government Organisation
OBV	Operation Black Vote
REC	Race Equality Council
RES	Race Equality Scheme
RRAA	Race Relations Amendment Act
SRB	Single Regeneration Budget
TEC	Training and Enterprise Council

Definitions

The terms 'civic engagement' and 'capacity building' – and, indeed, 'social inclusion' – are widely used, but sometimes misunderstood, or interpreted differently. The following definitions reflect our own understanding of the terms.

Civic engagement

Communities with the greatest and most diverse citizen participation are often resilient and strong. Engaging citizens to address common issues is essential for educated decision-making.
(The Sustainable Communities Network, USA [www.sustainable.org/creating/civic.html])

Capacity building

The term 'community capacity building' means different things to different people. We understand it as meaning developing the capacity and skills of the members of a community in such a way that they are better able to identify, and help meet, their needs and to participate more fully in society.

It is therefore concerned with:

- *providing opportunities for people to learn through experience – opportunities that would not otherwise be available to them; and*

- *involving people in collective effort so that they gain confidence in their own abilities and their ability to influence decisions that affect them.*
(The Charity Commission for England and Wales – 'The promotion of community capacity building', November 2000 [www.charity-commission.gov.uk/publications/rr5.asp#7])

Social inclusion

Social inclusion is the process by which efforts are made to ensure that everyone, regardless of their experiences and circumstances, can achieve their potential in life. To achieve inclusion, income and employment are necessary but not sufficient. An inclusive society is also characterised by a striving for reduced inequality, a balance between individuals' rights and duties and increased social cohesion.
(Centre for Economic and Social Inclusion, 2002 [www.cesi.org.uk/])

An introduction to The 1990 Trust

The 1990 Trust is a key Black non-government organisation. It was set up in 1990 by the National Black Caucus in order to create a policy influencing sister project, which could also have charitable status. Its work also emphasises giving support to, and capacity building within, Black communities in Britain, in order that they might directly participate in policy formation.[1]

One of the Trust's main priorities, therefore, is to ensure that Black communities are fully involved in the decisions that determine the life and health of these communities.

The Black Community and Voluntary Sector has been central to the rise of several known Black leaders (e.g. the late Bernie Grant, MP, Paul Boateng, MP and, in fact, most Black MPs). It has also, as this research has shown, been able to increase the involvement of hundreds of other Black people in local politics and the local economy.

It is central to the Trust's work to empower the Black Voluntary and Community Sector to support the work of social and political enfranchisement.

The Trust has tried to do this both through research such as this, which illustrates the issues affecting this particular part of the voluntary sector, and through direct support for community organisations (such as training schemes designed to empower participants with knowledge about how the political and social infrastructure of Britain is constructed, and the skills and confidence to challenge or engage).

The Trust was also active after the murder of Stephen Lawrence in supporting calls for the public inquiry and, indeed, was responsible for ensuring that Nelson Mandela, on a visit to Britain in 1993, made the call for an inquiry very public via extensive media coverage.

The 1990 Trust is a partner in a research consortium – the Race and Ethnic Diversity Research and Policy Partnership (REDRAPP) – with other NGOs and academic institutions.

For more information on The 1990 Trust see www.blink.org.uk.

1 Introduction and background

Introduction

This research project looks at the relationship between funding of the Black Voluntary and Community Sector (BVCS) and how this affects the ability of the sector to involve Black and Minority Ethnic (BME) communities in London and Leicester in civic engagement, social inclusion and capacity building (see 'Definitions' section at the front of this report for an explanation of these terms). The government is increasingly recognising the crucial role of the voluntary sector as a whole. In their foreword to the HM Treasury's (2003) report *futurebuilders*, Paul Boateng, Chief Secretary to the Treasury and Sir Michael Bichard, Chair of the Compact Working Group which worked with the Treasury on the report, state:

> The role of the voluntary and community organisations and social enterprises is central to this government's commitment to delivering world class public services. The sector is a crucial partner in working with central and local government to improve services for users. And the government equally has a key role in creating a climate and operating environment conducive to active participation.
> (HM Treasury, 2003, p. 5)

However, from the daily contact that The 1990 Trust has with Black groups, we had a different impression. We understood that many Black Voluntary and Community Sector groups, funders and other stakeholders believed that current funding arrangements were having a negative impact on the ability of such groups to meet their aims and objectives. While the *futurebuilders* report mentioned above recommends a fund of £125 million for the voluntary and community sector, this will be directed towards supporting service provision and not in building the sector in itself. The Treasury report states:

> Specifically, futurebuilders is about enhancing the capability of organisations delivering front line services, not about developing the wider service delivery role, nor about general voluntary sector development or infrastructure.
> (HM Treasury, 2003, p. 4)

Also, it is important that research, such as this study and that of McLeod *et al.* (2001), helps to illustrate the contribution that Black Voluntary and Community Sector groups can make to capacity building and social inclusion, and how this should be taken into account when shaping funding regimes.

Why this research was needed

The Black Voluntary and Community Sector plays a central and indispensable part in the daily lives of hundreds of thousands of Black members of society, no matter what their gender, class, beliefs or abilities. It delivers services to youth, seniors, disabled people and so on, through cultural, social and economic programmes. There are more than 3,000 Black non-government organisations in London and approximately 700 in Leicester. However, funding and resources to Black Voluntary and Community Sector have always been perceived by those in the sector as being at the mercy of political whim and circumstance.

The fluctuations in policy regarding funding for race relations matters have been the result of a range of initiatives that have followed various governments' attempts to deal with the perceived problems of immigrants since the 1950s.[1] These problems stemmed from the fact that Britain's immigration policies were based on the economic necessities of cheap labour and not the objective of social inclusion (Sivanandan, 1982). Social and human rights issues were never fully attended to. Therefore housing, education and health services were not prepared, appropriate or adequate to provide a reasonable and fair social context for the 'immigrants'.

From these very early days, the Black Voluntary and Community Sector needed to organise for its own needs.[2] It also formed partnerships for survival, such as banding together to buy properties in the face of the difficulties of obtaining mortgages and open colour bars from landlords and estate agents.[3] These organisations have always had a political underbelly; even where the organisation was apparently about social need, there was always an awareness of the climate of discrimination (Sivanandan, 1982).

With various new government initiatives and proposals in the pipeline, the ground appears to be set for further retreat from the support for focused and dedicated support to the self-organisation of Black communities. The reasons for this include the following.

- The creation of the Commission for Equalities and Human Rights which will eliminate the Commission for Racial Equality as a separate government entity focused on racial discrimination, potentially downgrading racism as a priority issue.

- The current political environment, which is calling for integration and cohesion, exemplified in the Ouseley report (Ouseley, 2001) from Bradford and the Cantle report from Oldham (Home Office, 2001). These lay much more emphasis on generic provision and service delivery than on the development of the Black Voluntary and Community Sector as a means of empowerment.

- The climate of racism in some elements of the media, which is echoed by some government officials (e.g. Home Secretary David Blunkett) regarding immigrants, refugees and asylum seekers.

This brief overview demonstrates that the fortunes of the Black Voluntary and Community Sector are inextricable from the politics of race in Britain. Since the 1970s, there has been a tangible retreat in funding this sector, as well as significant changes in how the funding process functions.

We believe the health of the sector is in danger of rapid deterioration. The level and sustainability of resources available to the sector determine its ability to continue and to expand its role as a primary deliverer of needed services. It also determines its ability to act as a driving force for effective civic engagement and participation.

From a number of vantage points – demographic, cultural, social, political, economic and legal – the UK is in transition in terms of its racial and ethnic composition and relations. The Black Voluntary and Community Sector must help communities to adapt to these changing analyses and demographics. It must also ensure that there are sufficient opportunities for people to become active, voting members of the community so that they can voice their own opinions on these developments.

The issue of funding for the Black Voluntary and Community Sector remains paramount in addressing these changes in British society. Ongoing and rigorous review and assessment of the situation, such as this research, are essential to monitor how this issue is addressed.

This research takes into account not only the current state of funding to the sector, but also the direction towards which the funding approach may have to head in the very near future.

Why Leicester and London?

The research focused on the Black Voluntary and Community Sector in London and Leicester for a number of reasons. First, they both have significant Black communities and are rich sources for examples of good and bad practice. Leicester has a reputation for high levels of civic engagement and good working relationships between Asian, African and Caribbean communities. In Leicester, there are significant and 'representative' numbers of local authority members but there are also disproportionate numbers of minority ethnic women local authority members.

London, on the other hand, is more known for an intense amount of Black political activity than for civic engagement and cross-community working relationships, and London's Black communities appear more dispersed.

It is projected in the 2001 census that, by 2011, Leicester will be the first UK city with a Black population above 50 per cent, a tremendous leap from the 28.1 per cent that existed in the 1991 census.[4] Currently, the Black and Minority Ethnic population in Leicester is 36 per cent. According to the 2001 census, London's Black and Minority Ethnic population constitutes about 28 per cent of the city.

Of the 11 London boroughs covered by this research, the Black and Minority Ethnic population as a percentage of the total was as shown in Table 1.

There is a great deal to be learnt from a study in these two cities, where all the vagaries of funding arrangements and allocations have sometimes had a ravaging effect on Black communities.

Nearly half (48 per cent) of Britain's total ethnic minority population lives in London including 78 per cent of Black Africans and 56 per cent of Bangledeshis.

Leicester provides a revealing model. According to the 2001 census, of the overall population, 29.92 per cent is Asian – representing about 85 per cent of all Black Minority Ethnic groups; 6.23 per cent is Black Caribbean, African, Chinese, mixed or 'Black other'.

Many groups are weary of battling with different rules, changing goalposts and constantly changing personnel.

In both London and Leicester, there is a long history of settled Black communities with deep roots in these areas. There has never been a period when there was not a Black presence in London. Although attention has rightfully focused on the post-World War II period, when massive numbers of Blacks and Asians came to the UK, they were greeted by existing, albeit smaller, communities and became part of that historic flow.

Another reason for choosing these cities was that the researchers had excellent access to the Black Voluntary and Community Sector in both of them. This included pivotal organisations and individuals such as the Black Londoners' Forum, which has a membership of 1,200 Black affiliated groups; Operation Black Vote (OBV); National Assembly Against Racism; and Lee Jasper, the London Mayoral Senior Adviser on Equalities. Steering group members included Rita Patel, a board member of East Midlands Development Agency and long-time activist in Leicester, and Joe Allen, Chair of the regional Community Fund board in the East Midlands.

Finally, Leicester and London provide rich sources of information and experiences because of the variety of Black Voluntary and Community Sector and non-BVCS groups in those two cities, funded and non-funded. This allowed the project to

Table 1 Black and Minority Ethnic population in the London boroughs covered by this research as a percentage of the total

Local authority	Black and Minority Ethnic population (% of total population)
Brent	54.7
Greenwich	22.9
Hackney	40.6
Haringey	34.4
Hillingdon	21.9
Lambeth	37.6
Southwark	37.0
Tower Hamlets	48.6

assess an extensive array of variables based on gender or faith. The researchers also drew from research recently completed in Milton Keynes (Chouhan and Jasper, 2000b) and ongoing work in Bedfordshire (Tomlins, 2003). Both of these studies have provided information on factors leading to low levels of civic engagement.

Previous reports

We drew on progress made in the development of *Black and Minority Ethnic Voluntary and Community Organisations: A Code of Good Practice* (Home Office, 2002). This follows the *Compact on Relations between Government and the Voluntary and Community Sector* (Home Office, 1998a). This study also builds on the government's report *Race Equality in Public Services* (Home Office, 2000) which reviewed ethnic minorities' involvement in their communities. We also cite two other important government reports:

- *Community Cohesion: A Report of the Independent Review Team,* also known as the Cantle Report (Home Office, 2001), which was written in the wake of the northern race riots of summer 2001

- *The Role of the Voluntary and Community Sector in Service Delivery: A Cross Cutting Review* (HM Treasury, 2002).

While recognising the need for communities to come together, the Cantle report – disproportionately in our view – put the onus on Black communities to integrate themselves into the broader populace. There was little emphasis given on the need for the UK general public to take responsibility for their own prejudices. It failed to give due recognition to the decades of organisation across cultural and religious divides within the Black Voluntary and Community Sector, which to a large extent has been a result of being disenfranchised by wider society.

The sector has a strong tradition of trying to ensure that the various minority communities can enjoy full citizenship rights and have the opportunity to be active in cohesive communities. In the *Cross Cutting Review* report (HM Treasury, 2002), it was acknowledged that the Black Voluntary and Community Sector experiences many of the same obstacles and problems as the larger voluntary sector, but more acutely. The government also admitted in the same paper that it had failed in its outreach efforts to the sector. This was compounded, we feel, by its limited perspective, seeing such groups primarily as service deliverers (see the HM Treasury [2003] report, *futurebuilders*, which was the result of the Treasury's *Cross Cutting Review* [HM Treasury, 2002].)

The National Council for Voluntary Youth Services' analysis (February 2002) of the *Cross Cutting Review* supports the view that the importance of the Black Voluntary and Community Sector does not lie solely in service provision. Groups within this sector are, as second-tier organisations, also change agents, political commentators and lobby groups. The Council's report argues that the members of the sector act as conduits for social inclusion and civic engagement. Black Voluntary and Community Sector organisations can reach excluded parts of society, which other organisations are less able to do, it suggests.

This research also refers to, and is informed by, the excellent publication by the Social Exclusion Unit (2000a), *Minority Ethnic Issues in Social Exclusion and Neighbourhood Renewal*, identifying issues such as qualifications and skills, employment, racist crime, health, housing and participation in neighbourhood renewal as important to these communities.

One strand of research developed by this project sought to identify – more from the vantage point of a case study approach than a quantitative one – differentials in funding levels and mechanisms between the voluntary sector as a whole and the Black Voluntary and Community Sector. Rather than attempting to amass all the available data on voluntary sector funding (a task beyond the scope of this research), this project identified several important funders and looked at their funding approaches. We also investigated the funders' understanding of capacity building, civic engagement and social inclusion – key concepts to this research (see 'Definitions' section at the front of this report).

Aims and objectives

The aims of this research were to:

- contribute to ensuring equitable (not equal) funding to the sectors

- contribute to the movement to ensure increased potential for capacity building, social inclusion and civic engagement in the sectors

- facilitate informed dialogue between the Black Voluntary and Community Sector, funders and other stakeholders.

This research sought to concentrate on three issues:

- the impact of the sector on civic engagement and social inclusion, including capacity building for individuals

- the degree to which local Black organisations perceive their position vis-à-vis funding and particularly the opportunities and operation of funding streams in supporting the above

- how funders relate to the sector.

Our objectives were to:

- identify perceived differentials in funding levels, purposes and methods for the Black Voluntary and Community Sector

- identify critical factors for social inclusion, civic engagement and capacity building

- identify blocks and barriers to the above

- inform future policy and practice towards the sector as a result of the findings.

Background to the funding of Black Voluntary and Community Sector organisations

The 1980s were witness to cuts in local authorities' equal opportunity units, and in the Black Voluntary and Community Sector and the voluntary sector generally. They also saw the denunciation of systemic attempts to tackle racism – exemplified by the derisory views expressed by Melanie Phillips (1993) in *The Observer* about CCETSW's (Central Council for Education and Training in Social Work's) Paper 30, 'Anti discriminatory practice in social work', which specified guidelines for anti-racist training in social work:

> *Courses teaching the new diploma in social work, the DipSW, must ensure students understand the processes of structural oppression, race, class and gender and 'ensure they are aware of individual and institutional racism and ways to combat both through anti-racist practice'. This profoundly illiberal gobbledegook has been laid down by CCETSW, the social workers' training body, in a document entitled Paper 30. If social work courses don't measure up to these dictates, they risk failing to be validated. Certain professors of social work have been fighting running battles with CCETSW on the grounds that such assumptions of structural oppression and racism are matters of opinion, not unshakeable fact.*
> (Phillips, 1993)

In the 1980s, the Conservative government, headed by Margaret Thatcher, continued to reinforce the denial of the structural nature of racism. Mrs Thatcher was particularly adamant that the fear of strangers and of swamping by non-

Whites was natural, as the following report of her comments, in the *Daily Mail*, illustrates:

> *If we went on as we are, then by the end of the century there would be four million people of the New Commonwealth or Pakistan here. Now that is an awful lot and I think it means that people are really rather afraid that this country might be swamped by people with a different culture. And, you know, the British character has done so much for democracy, for law, and done so much throughout the world, that there is a fear that it might be swamped, people are going to react and be rather hostile to those coming in.*
>
> (Daily Mail, 31 January 1978)

Many institutions and voluntary organisations thought this signalled a retreat from the goal of racial equality and perpetuated a denial of institutional or any kind of racism. Mrs Thatcher felt that anti-racism made things worse for Black people, just as sanctions in South Africa would hurt Black people (Chouhan and Jasper, 2000, p. 142).

In this climate, the Black Voluntary and Community Sector struggled to establish a platform for its own development, something that would need to receive significant funding. Several undaunted activists continued to make the case for Black empowerment – not, as the common view would have it, to simply create enclaves of resistance, but to ensure that empowerment meant being able to operate in and influence mainstream society in political, social and economic arenas.

The continuing denial of the structural nature of racism (Chouhan and Jasper, 2000) led to the causes of, and underlying factors behind, racism going unchecked. This in turn meant that the extent of racist activity and racist attacks was heeded only in ad hoc and sometimes superficial ways. The current government has been abysmal in its pronouncements and actions concerning asylum seekers and immigrants, the Iraq war and Palestine. It has refused to take on board the issue of reparations for slavery, raised at the World Conference against Racism in 2001, and has fuelled a racist backlash against the Lawrence inquiry, particularly as a result of David Blunkett's comments on 'swamping' and 'whingers' and denials of institutional racism. Its failure to address racism head on and lack of a consistent policy is, in our opinion, a decisive factor in the level of racism.

One theme that emerged from the Lawrence inquiry hearings was the critical view of many Black Voluntary and Community Sector groups that short-term, unsupported or inadequate funding led to unsustainable projects and, even worse, to accusations of failure by the sector to meet goals and objectives. This funding approach and subsequent changes, in turn, led to what was widely viewed as a decrease in the overall funding for the sector. This has been the perceived pattern of funding right across the sector for many years and has been an obstacle to overcoming marginalisation for individuals and groups. Appropriately, many believe that Black and Community Voluntary Sector groups are 'funded to fail'.

One key example of this, which emerged during the Lawrence Inquiry, was the fate of the various racial attacks monitoring projects run by voluntary organisations or in partnerships with local authorities. Many had their funding cut, partly because they were seen as too political. Yet, following the inquiry, there was an increasing call for more such projects. Research by Lemos and Crane (2000) led to the creation of Race Action Net and renewed calls for racial attacks monitoring from community-based projects. Also, as a result of the Inquiry, third-party reporting centres for racial attacks have been encouraged. These are very often Black community venues.

Importance of the Black Voluntary and Community Sector in Britain

From the earliest period of post-war migration and settlement, academic and policy interests have focused on the role and importance of the Black Voluntary and Community Sector. Early studies (Sivanandan, 1982) emphasised the part played by minority people themselves in setting up and finding support through their own organisations (for social, cultural, religious and economic purposes) as an alternative to the neglect, ignorance and prejudice they found in approaching the institutions of the so-called 'host society'.

Kofi Busia's study of the Black churches of Britain (1966) was an early precursor of a large number of similar books and articles, as well as an example of the quality of research that those same Black communities could themselves deliver. Alliances of Black organisations, such as the National Black Caucus and those who came together to hold the Agenda 2000 conference in Birmingham's International Convention Centre in October 1995, have continued to play an important role in mediating between these communities, their social exclusion and the institutions of the majority society.

Furthermore, such Black agencies have frequently provided the bulk of the welfare services received by members of those communities and a means by which the majority community agencies 'reach' them. It is therefore not entirely surprising that there have been a number of initiatives with local and national government and independent sector support to encourage the development of these community-based voluntary groups. These have included both direct and indirect support, such as the 'skills exchange fund' of the Baring Foundation, the Home Office support for the 'Resource Unit for Black Volunteering' and the support offered by the Self Help Alliance.

Research evidence, however, suggests that, despite the apparently benevolent intentions of many of these initiatives, support has not always been unequivocally beneficial for minority groups. It also suggests that funding under the Urban Programme (including Inner City Partnership and Training and Enterprise Councils as well as later initiatives) has frequently not been equitably distributed to Black and Minority Ethnic group-led agencies (see Joseph Rowntree Foundation *Findings* 227, 1997). The evidence points to a concern that minority organisations do not receive the level of support that their activity merits and that they require to operate at a fully effective level.

Official views and statements about Black communities are changing, in our view. This is partly as a result of consistent and persistent community organisation, which has argued that the pathological racist stereotyping must stop. It is also partly because openly recognising institutional racism is, we believe, in itself a powerful factor in changing perceptions and expressions of race matters.

The Stephen Lawrence inquiry defined institutional racism as:

> ... *the collective* failure of an organisation to provide an appropriate and professional service to people because of their colour, culture or ethnic origin. *It can be seen or detected in processes, attitudes and behaviour which amount to discrimination through unwilling prejudice, ignorance, thoughtlessness and racist stereotyping which disadvantage minority ethnic people.*
> (Stephen Lawrence Inquiry report, 1999, p. 28, emphasis added)

The murder of Stephen Lawrence was an illustration of the denial of the causes and maintaining factors of racism both prior to the murder, at the scene and afterwards. (Chouhan and Jasper, 2000).

While some enlightened authorities tried to implement equal opportunities policies before then, largely as a result of community pressure, most did not even bother to implement the statutory duty of the Race Relations Act 1976. The Commission for Racial Equality estimates only about 25 per cent of authorities ever used the general duty properly.

As a result of the inquiry, many institutions in Britain declared themselves institutionally racist and instigated diversity strategies. The Ofsted report 1999 (Raising the Attainment of Minority Ethnic Pupils; Schools and LEA responses) supported the view put forward by Sir Herman Ouseley, then Chair of the Commission for Racial Equality, that British schools were institutionally racist. It said it wanted to learn more about the communities it was serving and make its services more culturally appropriate.[5]

The Race Relations Amendment Act 2002 strengthened this movement by requiring 40,000 public authorities in England and Wales to meet a strengthened race equality duty and for the majority to produce race equality schemes. These schemes have a major requirement to assess the adverse impacts of their policies on different communities. To do this, it is necessary to know who those communities are and also something about them. Without this information, a high quality and useful impact assessment will be impossible.

Black Voluntary and Community Sector organisations under attack

However, while legislation and policy seemingly encourage public authorities to be supportive of communities, there are also contrary initiatives that send a different message. For example, in the new Nationality and Immigration Act (passed by parliament in November 2002), the government is quite open about the economic basis of its managed migration policy.

In arguing for support of the bill, the government, in the consultation paper for the Nationality and Immigration Act 2002, *Secure Borders Safe Haven*, asked:

What does the UK need to do to ensure that it has the people it needs to prosper in the world economy?

While, in the same consultation paper, there were discussions about citizenship classes and political rights, there was very little said about social and human rights and the responsibility that society has towards migrants – many of whom are being brought in to help the UK 'prosper in the world economy'.

At the same time, recent newspaper headlines such as 'New Labour gurus warn Blair to get tough on immigration' (*Guardian,* September 2002), make it clear to Black communities that the politics of race and immigration are still prevalent. The new Asylum and Immigration Bill going through Parliament in January 2004 is set to add even more draconian measures on asylum and immigration.

Since the publication of the Lawrence report, which should have marked a new era in anti-racism within the UK, we have seen the race riots in the North of England in the summer of 2001, which were fuelled by British National Party activity in the area.

There has been a racist backlash, which began from the publication of the Lawrence inquiry – such as the right-wing media and the Police Federation claiming the inquiry had gone too far (Chouhan and Jasper, 2000) – which has gathered pace.

On top of this, the terrorist attack on the World Trade Center on 11 September that year has led to increasing difficulties, particularly for the Muslim communities in the UK but also anyone who may stereotypically fit the bill. (For further details, see: *Islamophobia: A Challenge for Us All* by the Runnymede Trust, 1997 and 'Summary Report on Islamophobia in the EU after 11 September 2001', European Monitoring Centre, 2002.)

In May 2003, the far-right British National Party (BNP) was able to use a wave of anti-Muslim sentiment to win local council seats in Broxbourne, Burnley, Calderdale, Dudley, Sandwell and Stoke-on-Trent. In South Staffordshire, another far-right candidate from the Freedom Party, a split-off from the BNP, won a council seat. The BNP controls 16 local council seats in Britain, an unprecedented figure.

In 2002, many Black groups were again forced into anxiety about whether their Community Fund bids would even be considered in the light of the *Daily Mail* campaign against the National Coalition on Anti-deportation Campaign. The furore began when the National Lottery Charities Board allocated £340,000 to the Coalition, which had a statement on its web site that the government was 'colluding with fascism'. The *Daily Mail* and some government and political officials then sought – unsuccessfully – to cancel or stop renewal of funding to the organisation.

This controversy suggests that strong disagreement with particular government policies could be financially harmful, even if funding did not come from the government itself. Although, in this instance, the grant was upheld, it is feared within the Black Voluntary and Community Sector that the National Lottery Charities Board will be under pressure to judge applicants for funds on an increasingly politicised basis (Williams, 2002)

The new funding regime

A large number of researchers believe that many of the market values and ideologies that govern the funding machine clearly show preference to particular types of organisation – usually larger, more 'professionalised' organisations. In other words, the preference is for a Black Voluntary and Community Sector partner to have significant capacity to write reports as well as fluent financial and management systems. However, difficulties arise because these organisations do not have the same level of resources as public authorities in developing their capacity in order to adopt this new managerial approach.

This is a view that we recognise many small predominantly White-led organisations would share. However, it is particularly important for Black organisations, as they are trying to address a wider issue of social inclusion, rather than just providing a specific service for their community.

As public authorities take on and constantly adapt to new agendas (e.g. Best Value reviews, Investors in People) as part of the Modernising Government agenda, expectations of the voluntary sector rise. Yet, the expectation is totally disproportionate to the pace or desire at which the voluntary sector can adapt, understand or deal with the new regimes.

Writing in *The Guardian* in November 2000, journalist Julian Dobson suggested that the government's national strategy for neighbourhood renewal might not coincide with the aims of community organisations. He quoted a response from Community Matters, an umbrella group for local associations and campaigners, which made the point that there can be resentment by solely determining success in capitalistic criteria:

> *Community Matters is concerned with what it sees as an over-emphasis on individual, and in some cases external leadership (for example some of the references to social entrepreneurs and community leader training) ... It is our experience that communities resent such 'impositions', and function most effectively with democratic structures and collective decision making.*
> (Dobson, 2000)

The 'contract culture' has meant the Black Community and Voluntary Sector, despite being on the front lines in the fight against poverty and exclusion, is at risk of being overlooked by the very programmes that are supposed to address these issues. For instance:

- the introduction of the Single Regeneration Budget has severely affected the activities of Black groups

- the new funding regimes and criteria have made it increasingly difficult for many Black groups to obtain funding

- the Single Regeneration Budget amalgamated many smaller ad hoc funding streams, thereby closing some of the many avenues and opportunities for Black and Minority Ethnic organisations that previously existed, and setting up a rigorous and competitive application process.

As McLeod *et al.* (2001) state:

This was particularly important for Black and Minority Ethnic Organisations, as Home Office funds formerly earmarked specifically for assisting minority communities were thrown into the 'pot' without there being a requirement that they continue to benefit those communities.
(McLeod et al., 2001, p. 4.)

This means that programmes similar to the Single Regeneration Budget will be keen to emphasise the 'value for money' (low unit costs), quality standards (as accredited by mainstream bodies), rigorous monitoring and evaluation (increased paperwork) creed of their predecessor. McLeod (1996, p. 6) backs this by stating that the Black Voluntary and Community Sector is likely to experience increasing difficulties in accessing the resources it requires for tackling the real problems of poverty and disadvantage.

However, there are organisations that survive and flourish in this context, and are keen to emphasise the value of financial self-sufficiency. One of the main texts examined in this research (McLeod *et al.*, 2001) also illustrates how:

Larger voluntary organisations, who have the clout to develop more formulaic approaches, tend to do much better on 'contract compliance', by having 'proper' accounting procedures, service standards, management systems.
(McLeod et al., 2001, p. 5)

The other side to this argument is that smaller, grass-roots organisations with few or no paid staff cannot take advantage of such a funding process. Nonetheless, to cite McLeod *et al.* (2001), Black and Minority Ethnic Organisations (BMEO) also have:

… neither the historical and organisational links of the White-led voluntary organisations, or the organisational structure nor experience to negotiate their way successfully through the new contract regime.
(McLeod et al., 2001, p. 5)

Gender and the Black Voluntary and Community Sector

These policies also have a gender dimension. Black women in the sector who we spoke to were very often in managerial or administrative roles and dealt with the ins and outs of contract compliance on a daily basis. However, this expertise was often not recognised or used to best advantage. In addition, it emerged that, while Black women head up many Black Voluntary and Community Sector projects and very often are those ensuring the sustainability of the projects, it is men who seem to be projected in the public eye, or involved in the 'parts of the work which involve the high level meetings and press conferences'.

Sonia Davis and Veronica Cooke (2002) examine the extent to which current funding policies and arrangements reflect the stated needs and principles of Black women's organisations. Like many of the other studies cited in this report, they also argue that the process of funding takes place in a very competitive arena of application (Davis and Cooke, 2002, p. 25).

That report highlights systematic mechanisms of funding that the authors believe stunt the well-being of women-led Black Voluntary Sector organisations. They suggest that the absence of any clear policy or strategy relating specifically to the funding of Black women's organisations underlies the failure to explain different funding levels and the mismatch 'between expectations, funding levels and capacity of the organisations' (Davis and Cooke, 2002, p. 21).

The authors note that the local government officials they interviewed had a tendency 'to see Black women's organisations as a distinctive section within the voluntary sector, servicing a distinct need'. They also saw them as being instrumental in enabling 'social inclusion and civic engagement, thus fitting into the key strategies and policies of the local authorities on social inclusion and its variants' (Davis and Cooke, 2002, p. 25).

Yet these insights were not reflected in the funding of the projects. Davis and Cooke (2002) also found that, of the 14 case study organisations, only two had received monies from the Single Regeneration Budget, one had received some from Health Action Zone funding and two had some form of New Deal for Communities funding. However, most importantly:

No non-funded organisations had managed to tap into partnership schemes and no new organisational areas within the Black women's voluntary sector had been created.
(Davis and Cooke, 2002, p. 31)

Gender perspectives within the sector are therefore extremely pertinent. It is a fallacy that African or Asian women are too busy with family to want to get involved. In fact, to the contrary, they welcome the opportunity to know how they get their needs met from the system because they are so concerned about the welfare of their families and communities.[6]

The Black Voluntary and Community Sector and civic and political engagement

Black-led voluntary organisations across the board enable Black and Minority Ethnic individuals to participate in public life and the sector empowers users through involvement in the design and execution of services. These organisations are also a key factor in the alleviation of poverty and are keen

advocates on community needs. Even the Home Office acknowledges they 'actively involve some of the most socially excluded people and communities in England' (Home Office, 1998b, p. 4). Some organisations openly avowed empowerment and enfranchisement of the Black communities as one of their main aims. One such group is Operation Black Vote.

A study commissioned by the Electoral Commission and Operation Black Vote (Ward, 2002) revealed that you cannot redress democratic deficit by simple changes in electoral procedures proposed by the government. You had to address issues of Black representation. The survey found that 43 per cent of Black Britons named 'better representation of Blacks in politics' as a condition more likely to encourage them to vote. Only 4 per cent claimed that moves to make voting easier or more convenient were a motivator to get involved in the electoral process.

A key factor to bear in mind is that formal politics weigh heavily in favour of middle-class Whites. With only 12 Black MPs (out of 659 MPs) many Black people feel, justifiably, that they are under-represented in the political system. They also feel that, at present, their views and voices cannot be and are not heard through these institutions.

There are other means by which many individuals have sought to deal with their concerns outside of formal institutions. Operation Black Vote (OBV) argues that, to enable the direct involvement in party politics by Black Britons, we must first ensure their capacity to do this by encouraging civic engagement in many other aspects of life. OBV has therefore instituted shadowing schemes for school governors, magistrates and MPs as one example of how this can be done. It also works in partnership with other Black Voluntary and Community Sector groups on capacity-building training, providing general learning about how the system works and how to get the best from it.

Other political leaders, such as MEP Claude Moraes, have encouraged and worked hard to get

Black citizens involved in European Union issues and even to become MEP candidates. There are currently only four Black British MEPs out of 87 representatives.

Why this study is important

As the foregoing overview demonstrates, there is a vivid and vital need for this study. It is apparent that:

- the levels of civic engagement (representation in employment, on public bodies as councillors and politicians, etc.) is disproportionate to the numbers of Black people in the UK and this is reflected to a varying extent on a regional basis (e.g. 12 Black MPs out of 659 MPs)

- the levels of disaffection and social exclusion are disproportionate for the Black community (see Box 1).

Box 1   Indicators of social exclusion

Housing

- More than half of Pakistani and Bangladeshi households and one-third of Black Caribbean households are in the 10 per cent most deprived wards in England, compared to only 14 per cent of White households.

- About one-third of Pakistani and Bangladeshi households live in unfit properties, compared to about 6 per cent of White households.

- In London, between June and September 2000, 49 per cent of households accepted as homeless by local authorities were from ethnic minorities. Of these, 23 per cent were from African and Caribbean

(continued)

---

households, although they comprise only 11 per cent of households in London. (Source: 1990/2000 Survey of English Housing, DTLR; 1996 English House Condition Survey, DTLR, quoted in Performance and Innovation Unit, Cabinet Office, 2001.)

Employment

- Minority ethnic unemployment is more than double that of comparable White groups and people from minority ethnic communities are more adversely affected than the White population when unemployment increases as a result of economic downturns.

- In 2001, 5 per cent of White men were unemployed compared with 13 per cent of Black African or 9 per cent Afro-Caribbean men, 7 per cent of Indian, 16 per cent of Pakistanis and 20 per cent of Bangladeshi men. (Sources: Performance and Innovation Unit, Cabinet Office, 2001; 2001 census.)

On the basis of these figures, the Policy and Innovation Unit of the Cabinet Office has concluded:

Given the evidence that has been presented it is undeniable that racial harassment and racial discrimination persist in the UK labour market.

Education

- Black Caribbean pupils are four times more likely to be excluded from school compared to White pupils (DfES, 2002, 2003).

- Indian and Chinese/other Asian pupils do better than their White counterparts. (Performance and Innovation Unit, Cabinet Office, 2001, p. 5; DfES, 2003).

(continued)

- Bangladeshi, Black and Pakistani pupils in particular achieve less well than others – many of these children enter the school system with equal ability to White children, but underachieve progressively as they go through the school system (Performance and Innovation Unit, Cabinet Office, 2001).

A recent Audit Commission (2002) report, undertaken jointly with Ofsted, showed that, in Tower Hamlets, London, the achievement of Bangladeshi children has significantly improved.

We build an evidence base in this research to show the following.

- The Black Voluntary and Community Sector is vital for the encouragement of social inclusion and civic engagement.

- While there are hundreds of Black Voluntary and Community Sector groups, many are caught up in service delivery and in trying to establish levels of sustainability. Hence, their potentially important contribution to the civic engagement and social inclusion is diminished.

In addition, we assess how funding and resources issues help or hinder these organisations.

A Black perspective

As a team of Black researchers, we have deliberately approached this research from a Black perspective. By this, we mean that we believe that social science research is never neutral or without perspective. This does not mean that objective criteria and research tools cannot be employed and, in fact, we would strongly argue that solid scholarly principles should be applied. A Black perspective applied in this context refers to ensuring that a Black voice is not erased or suppressed but helps to inform and articulate the analysis. The research incorporates the lived and perceived experiences of the subjects or issues being studied.

We believe that, while there is no one Black perspective, there is a collective experience, both historic and contemporary, shared by UK African, Caribbean and Asian communities. Through the cauldron of these experiences, important insights have emerged that have too often been absent from the research specifically focused on these communities. A Black perspective or approach rejigs and incorporates this experience into the analysis. It challenges the notion that there is 'value-free' research. We chose consciously to incorporate the views and opinions of the Black community voices into the preparation, implementation and summing up of this project. This approach did not exclude other views but guaranteed that a full array of diverse perspectives was included.

2 Methodology

Focus groups and questionnaires

There were two elements to this research: focus groups among organisations seeking funding and a questionnaire to funders of those organisations.

Focus groups

We held focus groups within the communities to find out what the Black Voluntary and Community Sector thought about their access to funding and the impact of funding on their contribution to capacity building, social inclusion and civic engagement in Black and Minority Ethnic communities. We did not accept the view of mainstream commentators that, while representation of Black communities is disproportionately low in many public and private arenas, Black communities are disenfranchised because they simply do not wish to participate.

While it is important to emphasise that this was not a quantitative research project, a large number of Black Voluntary and Community Sector groups, funders and other stakeholders were interviewed, surveyed, or otherwise contacted.

In total, nearly 57 Black Voluntary and Community Sector groups participated in focus group discussions. Thirty agencies returned the questionnaire. Approximately 200 individuals from groups and institutions from 14 areas in two cities were involved (eight areas in London and six in Leicester). We believe we obtained candid discussions and frank comments regarding the issue of funding for the sector and civic participation.

Questionnaires

As part of the research for this project, 150 questionnaires were sent out to civic and public bodies, funders and other related stakeholders who are involved with the Black Voluntary and Community Sector. This included local councils, health agencies, police services, private foundations, public funders and educational institutions. The questionnaires were divided into four parts, which covered organisational details, funding information, non-funding involvement with the Black Voluntary and Community Sector and representation of Black and Minority Ethnic individuals on the staff and boards of those being surveyed. Experienced researchers in consultation with BME groups and individuals developed the questionnaire.

The questionnaire was mailed to organisations and institutions in both London and Leicester, the two cities where the study was conducted. In addition, follow-up phone calls were made to determine if the questionnaire had been received, whether any clarifications were needed and if the recipient wanted it on disk.

The recipients were asked to fill out the forms and to add any other materials they felt would help illuminate or explain their answers. The forms were then sent back to the researchers. A select group of respondents were called and then later interviewed in person by a member (or members) of the research team. Interviews took place in London and in Leicester. The interviews helped to complement written responses and allowed those most involved in the funding of BVCS groups to expand ideas and reflections.

We employed a number of research methods to collect data for this project. These included:

- a content analysis from civic bodies' information on funding, representation and social inclusion

- desktop and library research in scholarly journals

- community-based meetings with the voluntary sector using a short questionnaire

- distribution of an in-depth questionnaire to a number of key funders and stakeholders

- interviews with key informants from the voluntary sector and civic bodies.

Outreach methods

The presentation and analysis in this report is based on desktop research, personal interviews, data from focus groups, responses to a questionnaire and, where relevant, individual case studies.

In the preliminary stage of the research, a questionnaire was developed based on desktop research into previous studies on this or related topics, discussions with relevant stakeholders and the comprehensive experiences of the research team.

Our initial research helped to identify organisations and institutions important to the issue – including Black Voluntary and Community Sector organisations and the institutions that fund them. We identified and contacted Black Voluntary and Community Sector groups to participate in the focus groups. As a result of this process, 57 BVCS groups took part in focus group discussions, with a total of approximately 170 individuals.

At the same time, questionnaires were sent to groups that were involved in some way in the funding, directly or indirectly, or resource provision to the Black Voluntary and Community Sector. These were sent out to around 150 organisations and institutions. As others have noted (McLeod *et al.*, 2001), the use of mail questionnaires to the Black Voluntary and Community Sector has not returned the kind of results that researchers sought to achieve.

Follow-up phone calls were made to some of these groups and, in some instances, personal interviews were held, again in London and Leicester, with staff representatives. These interviews provided additional data and insights both orally and in written form. Thirty agencies returned the questionnaire.

At least 200 individuals in groups and institutions from 14 areas in two cities were therefore involved (eight areas in London and six in Leicester).

The organisations selected for the focus groups were those whose primary or sole remit was to address issues of concern in Black communities. These area-based focus group meetings provided critical and previously unacknowledged insights into how Black Voluntary and Community Sector groups perceive their relationship to the funding community and how it affects their ability to do their work. They provided information on what is needed for social inclusion and capacity building, what would encourage more civic engagement, and views about levels and methods of funding. These meetings were often intense but always engaged.

Each group attending the meetings was asked to fill out a simple questionnaire at the meeting and the questions acted as a guide to the framework for discussions. Some of the questions focused on where, when, why and how the group started and in what way they have developed. We also discussed the role of key individuals and other positions they hold on voluntary or civic bodies.

The focus groups

The focus groups were vital to the research in that they sought to identify issues relating to funding, capacity building, civic engagement and social inclusion from Black perspectives. Eight areas of London[1] were targeted and six in Leicester.

In each area, there were between two and four focus groups (to ensure the range of views from women and men, young and old, faith groups and disability). A total of 57 groups were represented. With an average of three people per group consulted, the research reached over 170 individuals in London and Leicester. Most groups (excluding ten who did not want to be named) are listed in Appendix 3.

Areas were chosen for the range and density of Black populations. In Leicester, two areas (Braunstone and Humberstone) and, in London, two boroughs (Greenwich and Hillingdon) were chosen for their comparatively low numbers of Black people to act as comparators. In these areas, some White-led organisations also attended the focus groups.

We identified and trained community-based researchers in London and Leicester to help carry out the research involving the focus groups. These researchers were drawn from people who lived and/or worked in the areas identified and who we also knew to be reliable people capable of doing the work. We paid them for their training and per focus group. The benefits of using this methodology are that the community researchers have greater knowledge of the detail of the communities and can search out what others may deem hard to reach, whereas in fact it may be only that it is hard for them to hear.

We developed a set of questions with the researchers to help identify issues. These questions were sent to the groups with a letter of invitation to an arranged venue. They could either bring completed forms to the meeting, or fill them up at the meeting with help from the facilitator. However, in the end, all the questionnaires were filled up at the meetings. In some instances, language skills of the researchers were important; in others, the people attending were able to help each other. The questionnaire was only in English as, by and large, it went to organisers of groups who had no problems with English. But the researcher would check by phone who might be coming to the meetings and it was here that language skills were useful – especially with groups of Asian women.

We have merged the findings from London and Leicester in Chapter 3, except where we identify examples from each city. A list of groups that participated and agreed to be named can be found in Appendix 3. Understandably, many of the individuals in the groups did not want to be identified, as they thought it might jeopardise their funding in the future. Therefore Appendix 3 should be read as a sample list of groups to give an idea of the range.

3 Black Voluntary and Community Sector views – reports from the focus groups

There were five areas of questioning in the focus groups:

- background to the organisations

- funding

- accountability

- issues of inequality

- civic engagement, capacity building and social inclusion.

We address these in turn below.

Background to the organisations

The organisations were asked about the length of time they had been in existence, the funding they received, management committees and staff, aims and objectives.

The groups responding represented a very eclectic range of interests and platforms. Three London-based groups were national campaigning organisations (Operation Black Vote, the National Assembly Against Racism and the Confederation of Indian Organisations). Black women's groups and disabled groups were well represented, including one aimed particularly at refugees. Some were for very specific groups of people (e.g. Cypriot blind people's group), while others were aimed at Asian or African Caribbean communities across the geographical area.

This diversity within Black Voluntary and Community Sector groups is one of the key features of the vibrancy of the sector. Although there were key differences in aims and philosophy of participants, there was also a convergence around the general aim of challenging racism and discrimination.

Most had Black-led management committees and several employed workers, including White workers. People on committees included local councillors, lecturers, accountants, consultants, teachers, lawyers, health professionals, local residents and past clients. In most, there was a heavy reliance on voluntary effort.

Many recognised the importance of ensuring that local people were in the majority on committees. However, they also recognised that skills gaps sometimes needed to be filled from outside of the area, but by a person who had an established reputation in that field.

Funding

Perhaps unsurprisingly, the groups felt there was insufficient funding. However, this general view masked a wide range of issues.

Most groups realised the importance of diversifying sources of funding. However, there was a nervousness about moving between funders – especially where groups had worked hard on building up a relationship and understanding of the project's aims.

In addition, diversifying funding sources also meant that there were a number of different evaluation and monitoring procedures, and this acted as a heavy burden, especially for some of the smaller groups.

The variety of sources included the Home Office, local authorities, the BBC, the Community Fund, Comic Relief, Charitable Trusts, private companies and Single Regeneration Budget (SRB) funding. McLeod et al.'s research (2001) pointed to the fact that two-thirds of the funding for the sector came from central or local government or other statutory body (see Chapter 4).

One particularly successful initiative that we looked at was the Peepul Centre in Leicester, which is currently being built (see case study 1 below). It completed a match-funding jigsaw for a grant of £7 million from the Millennium Commission. Other sources included the Arts Council, SRB, Sport

England, East Midlands Development Agency, the Community Fund and the New Opportunities Fund. The Centre will operate on a business plan to become self-financing within five years and therefore free of the dependency on statutory funding.

Because of the vast experience of fund-raising and funding issues that the Peepul Centre has amassed, it is being used as a specific case study alongside one other organisation, which did not wish to be named. The latter is an African Caribbean led group in London. When comments are being made about these case studies, they will be indicated as case study 1 (Peepul Centre) and case study 2 (African Caribbean group).

The application process

The main issues around application processes concerned the apparently ever-changing procedures and the different requirements for every funder. Application forms differed from funder to funder, as did funding cycles:

> *Many groups perceived that the goalposts always seemed to be changing. Individual funding bodies often reviewed their procedures as well as the issue of no real cross-referencing between them.*
> (Focus group 6 facilitator report)

It was felt that some funders ask questions to which there are 'key phrases' that need to be used in response and only those 'in the know' would be able to use the correct jargon. For example, a funder looking for innovative learning initiatives asked about accreditation, learning portfolios and learning outcomes. Some organisations might have such innovative learning programmes but be put off by the jargon. Other groups were unsure about equal opportunity sections if they thought they needed to say they were open to all but in fact were women's groups or single issues groups.

Although groups felt that the processes of application to charities and other statutory providers were generally clear-cut and reasonable,

the same could not be said of the local council in one London borough and in one area of Leicester. Many Black and Minority Ethnic groups may not be in the 'loop' of what is happening locally, or because of the lack of transparency of the process. They feel they are always at a disadvantage compared with mainstream organisations that often have prominent local influential people on the council (Focus group 11).

Many complained that they did not always get feedback on why their grant application was rejected:

> *When they do respond it is the standard response – that of spreading the money wider.*
> (Focus group 1)

Many groups reported that there was an over-emphasis on Black groups not being discriminatory and that there was insufficient understanding of the principles and philosophy of self-organisation for minority groups.

In some instances, especially for larger grant amounts, there were two or three stages to the application. The last stages often involve assessors visiting the group. Some of the groups felt they had to spend too much time explaining context because of the assessor's lack of cultural knowledge. Even then, it was not always understood.

Box 2   Case study 1

The group were repeatedly questioned in their funding application about how they would reach the whole community and how they would overcome resistance. They were also asked about how their business plan would stack up if the whole community did not use the centre.

The reply was that it was for the whole community and, because Asian women ran it, that did not mean that others in the community would not use it. The group felt

(continued)

that stereotypical views of Asian women and Asian communities were brought to bear.

It was also interesting that the group reported that almost all the funders they had approached had refused a grant in the first instance. It was only by the group questioning the reasons for refusal and repeatedly going back to them that they eventually got funding. The Millennium Commission was one of those who refused initially but then eventually gave the £7 million that the project needed in order to start the process of getting match funding.

The following statement taken from recent documentation from the Peepul Centre illustrates the issues they faced:

More care and attention should be made to match assessors to projects. We have experienced times to date where assessors have come to the project with baggage from previous experiences that have had a very detrimental effect on the way our applications have been processed. We have also had concerns where assessors do not have experience of the communities they are assessing, and therefore wittingly or unwittingly are subtly undermining the community that is being specifically targeted for funding.

In the case of Black communities, they are set up as priorities for funding and then this undermining process from lack of understanding, whether intentional or not, results in failure of a bid with potential. In our case funding is needed in order to provide a service that is led by the community, and is culturally sensitive. Distributors are supporting us, as they know that existing strategies and programmes are failing to deliver because of a lack of understanding of the key issues, and the lack of understanding of the Black communities served. We wish to work in partnership to overcome these

(continued)

barriers, but find that we are being assessed and in some cases damned by people who do not have this wider perspective.

We also feel that there has often been a lack of clarity on behalf of the funders when seeking information, as they have not always known what they are looking or asking for. We become the victims of the distributors' learning curve – when you multiply this with the numbers of different distributors, it ends up being a hell of a disadvantage. We therefore feel that there should be more spent to help individual projects to a successful outcome, done on the basis of working in partnership. This support is needed in order to gain trust, and to overcome the concern that projects have that they are not being handled properly and indeed worry that they are being dealt with by a mentality of being set up to fail.

Appropriate and inappropriate funders

Groups were asked if there are certain funders to whom they would: (a) never apply, or (b) definitely apply.

Several said they would not accept money from tobacco companies, pharmaceutical companies, or companies that were openly exploitative in developing world countries. However, they admitted this was sometimes hard to determine – because of world politics, there were many links back to how developing nations were supported or not. For example Coca-Cola or Nike, whose products are enormously popular among Black communities, also make good use of cheap labour in developing world countries.

Two groups cited an umbrella group for minority ethnic organisations as a body they would never accept funding from, as they felt this would be a compromise of their principles. Many groups would like not to be so dependent on local authorities or government grants, as they felt it curbed their activities – believing that, if they were openly critical, they might subsequently have their funding cut the following year.

Some groups were emphatic that they would not change what they did to get funding. However, nearly all agreed that they had to word applications carefully to ensure that the funder's criteria were met.

Most organisations stated that they have had to change the way they packaged their services to meet new funding criteria. Others stated that they have had to totally refocus their services in terms of prioritising service provisions because of cuts:

We set up projects that were not a priority.
(Focus group 3)

Funding from charities or trusts

Very few of the groups had approached trusts or charities for funding. But, of those that had, most found these very helpful.

Several groups cited the Allen Lane Foundation, Barrow Cadbury Trust, Churches' Commission for Racial Justice, Joseph Rowntree Charitable Trust and Stone Ashdown Trust as trusts that seemed genuine in wanting to do something about racism. They were seen as supportive and helpful, and monitoring and accountability obligations were never excessive. Groups reported that they felt trusted and it made them feel as though they wanted to do the very best possible job.

Trusts were also more likely to fund for more than one year at a time and could ask for specific board decisions to suit a particular circumstance. However, there was a general lack of knowledge about the trusts and funding available.

> **Box 3 Case study 2**
>
> *When we were awarded funding by [a trust] ... it was so refreshing. The letter of grant was so enthusiastic, offered support and set out clearly what they needed, a quarterly report on progress and a visit from an officer and annual returns at the end of the year. It's*
>
> *(continued)*

just great when a funder seems to be working with you. We don't even mind putting their logo on leaflets and things because they should get some of the credit. They put their money where their mouths are and they have just as much interest in seeing it work as we do.

What we find most annoying is when a funder expects you to be eternally grateful and never say a word against them again, or think you are at their beck and call. This is a simple exercise of power by buying favour.

Use of fund-raisers

A large number of the groups would have liked to use fund-raisers but either could not afford them or did not know how to judge whether they would be able to deliver. One participant stated:

Some good, some dreadful – don't understand campaigning.
(Focus group 3)

In addition, many funders openly stated that they would not accept applications from fund-raisers.

It was suggested that a further piece of research could put together a list of fund-raisers with a tiered 'accreditation'. Tier 1 could be those with proven track records and good references as well as providing good value for money; tier 2 could be those with good credentials, but still building their profile. The lists would show fees or percentage payments. All of these could be interviewed and vetted by the researchers before they were put onto a list. The list could be accompanied by guidance on what to ask, letters of contract and other relevant matters.

Box 4   Case study 1

The group decided early on to go for the best fund-raisers in the field and in the process to get some training for themselves. A trainer was able to demonstrate the build-up and stages to an application or other ways of raising money, which all led finally to the big 'ask'. The fund-raisers that were brought in were expensive and, in all but one case, White men. So the group were concerned that their understanding of the organisation would not be good. However, because the group were very clear about the ethos, values and principles, they found that these men worked really well with the project and were so committed to it that they also worked at risk and sometimes for free. It was vital, however, that the group ensured that they read everything before it went out and that the fund-raisers knew that everything had to be checked back.

It has been very interesting for the group to see the developmental process of a fund-raiser – from someone who, at a first meeting, was perhaps sceptical of the project to someone who was an eyes-opened, tuned-in advocate.

Box 5   Case study 2

The group raised some money from a benevolent trust fund for a half-time fund-raiser, both parties believing that the fund-raiser would be worth the outlay for the money they would raise. However, things did not quite work out.

As the fund-raiser was an employee, by the time the group realised things were not working out, all the group could do was to

(continued)

terminate the employment, which luckily for them had been funded for only a year.

The group felt that, for this reason, they would have preferred to have used a fund-raiser who worked on a commission-only basis. Should the application have failed, the fund-raiser would have received a small flat fee, so that the group would at least have had some guarantees and safeguards. They could also have chosen never to use the person again and the outlay would have been small.

Sustainability and core funding

All had difficulty with sustainable funding and core funding. Many funders would only fund projects and would also bear some administrative and management costs. However, applying to funders for rent or key development workers – especially beyond a one-year term – was extremely difficult.

Some organisations were also caught in the bind that they would rather buy property and have an asset base than rent, as rent rates were exorbitant – especially in London. However, getting mortgages was difficult without the prospect of regular income, which very few voluntary organisations, if any, could offer. Some organisations were joining forces to share premises and to look for longer-term funding strategies for sharing facilities.

Despite the cash injection to Black and Minority Ethnic groups after the inner-area riots in the 1980s, these organisations soon learnt that cash without infrastructure and sound financial and organisational management experience was, in effect, funding for failure.

Many people in Leicester told of groups that had sprung up in a wave of expectation and optimism and then had been killed off by the inability to develop proper accounting systems and the weight of the management tasks. This was very damaging to the growth of the Black Voluntary and Community Sector and the relationship between funders and receivers.

Several key workers were constantly worried about finding rent and salaries, and spent up to half their time just trying to fund-raise. The problem here is that it leaves little time for delivering on services and, as a consequence, workers were stretching their working hours to in excess of 50 hours per week. Alternatively, they were not always able to deliver on already ambitious programmes and would then be seen as 'failing'. This further exemplifies the 'funding for failure' scenario.

One London borough has been working on a three-monthly budgetary funding cycle to Black and Minority Ethnic (BME) groups in the borough. This has limited groups' abilities to match fund, to develop services and their abilities to employ staff – many of who are currently employed on a month-to-month basis (focus group 9):

> The crucial problem is that, unlike many BME groups, mainstream organisations are being protected by being provided with a three-year ring-fenced contract. Some BME groups expressed the view that the council has developed a cultural exclusion strategy against the Black community.
> (Focus group 10 facilitator report)

> The money comes late and there is difficulty then to deliver fast under pressure without money. There was one time they asked us for the first progress report and we hadn't had the money yet, they were late with the forms but we were supposed to have delivered somehow on hot air. Without a cushion organisation, it would have been impossible.
> (Focus group 4)

One participant argued that, at some point, it is necessary for funders to take a leap of faith and put trust in an organisation to counter institutional racism and institutional caution:

> We had to convince funders we were stable before they would fund us but it was difficult to be stable without funding.
> (Focus group 5)

The point about cushion organisations, which provide cash up front until agreed funding comes through, is an important one. Very often, funders give grant money only in arrears, but many organisations, even the bigger ones, are on such tight cash flows that they cannot spend before the money comes in. Charities are not allowed to be overdrawn and so this puts them in a further bind.

Organisations that are able to help with the up-front payments or stand as guarantors are sometimes vital and more umbrella bodies or people willing to do this should be identified. One suggestion was that grant-givers should pay in advance, even if it were on a month-to-month basis for the first quarter. Then, once they were satisfied about accounting, they could pay the rest up front for the year.

The other crucial role for umbrella or cushion organisations is that they can provide financial management and other managerial expertise. We believe more of these initiatives should be funded.

Box 6   Case study 1

The Peepul Centre was a prime example of an organisation that had been dependent on local authority funding for several years. As such, it was subject to ad hoc cuts and constant politicking, and could not raise any extra cash, as this would always be 'clawed' back so that it could be offset against grant provision.

The group had for some time been operating from two small terraced houses as the Belgrave Baheno (sisters) organisation. It had started life as the Belgrave Girls' Youth Movement (BGYM) in 1979 and, after four years, received inner-area programme

(continued)

funding in an 'minority ethnic package' following the street riots and disturbances of 1981. The group were lucky. Founder members included two women who had previously been in banking and so, from the outset, excellent financial systems and accountability were in place. In addition, they had volunteers with key skills in management and community development work and, with an almost instinctual vision of where they wanted to go, they set about self-training.

One of their members commented:

In BGYM we learned our politics on the street. In the uprisings of 1980 and 1981 many young women were on the front lines or organising support. We realised that this was no way to go on, there had to be a better way to get the resources and the equality we needed and were entitled to.

We set up training course for ourselves and worked with African, Caribbean and Asian groups across the city. These courses were fantastic, as they brought together men and women, younger and older, African Caribbean and Asian sometimes for the first time.

We invited councillors, police, MPs, etc. and, to our surprise, they came. They sometimes seemed much more afraid of us than we could imagine but they had never been invited before and the dialogues were tough and sometimes fractious but we always made a point of ending in a positive way. As a result, we have African Caribbean and Asian partnerships to this day and many of the original trainees have gone on to become local councillors, directors, lecturers and some have stayed in the voluntary sector.

This self-training was continued until the group reached the point when they knew the only way forward was to aim at self-sufficiency. They asked the local authority if they could use some savings from the annual

(continued)

grant towards a feasibility study. The local authority said 'no' and this one decision, in the group's view, illustrated the short-sightedness and a lack of belief in the role and capability of the voluntary sector. It would also benefit the council to have the group removed from local authority dependency.

The group believe that this decision was in part politically motivated, as there were so few women on the council. Many of them, including Asian men, felt threatened by the idea of a voluntary sector group doing such 'grown-up things', which may go beyond the control of the local authority. However, the group did not take no for an answer and got the feasibility money that launched them into a six-year struggle to realise the dream of the Peepul Centre.

Strategic partnerships

Those interviewed recognised the increasing necessity to apply through partnerships. For one group, which exists to build broad alliances against racism, strategic partnerships were the main ways of working. This group favoured alliances with trades unions. However, there was some unease about partnerships in other areas. Some felt:

- partnerships with local authorities or other statutory bodies could compromise the independent nature of the organisation

- local authorities or other bodies would often say they were seeking full participation in partnerships, but actually wanted this only at a superficial level that did not involve a place at the decision-making table.

Margaret O' Rawe (1997) in her book *Human Rights on Duty* outlines principles for better policing in Northern Ireland. She discusses the various levels of participation by the community in policing matters. She includes a ladder graph used by Sherry Arnstein (1969) in her article 'A ladder of citizen participation' to illustrate this (see Figure 1).

Partnerships were not always equal. Where they were initiated by local authorities, this often meant that the local authorities could say they were working with groups, but, in reality, the relationship had only just been kicked off by the grant application. In addition, the agendas and objectives, resources and decision-making powers may be completely imbalanced.

This is akin to the failings of the multi-agency approach in some instances (Bowling, 2000). This covers a number of general issues, including funding. Different agencies come to the issue from different perspectives and, despite good intentions, have difficulty getting past discussions about the differences. Several groups mentioned experiencing the lack of understanding from partners or potential partners, for example:

The general feeling expressed about strategic partnership was, although it may be a good objective to aim for, it can only take place in an atmosphere where genuine partnership takes place, but not where the local authority acts as both a partner and a competitor at the same time.
(Focus group 8)

Figure 1 Levels of participation by the community in policing matters

High power
Controls
Helps design service
Partner
Participant
Involved
Consulted
Informed
Placated
Manipulated
Low power
Powerless

Source: Arnstein (1969).

A couple of the projects commented that they were often in conflict with the local authority in terms of developing strategic partnership in regards to service development. They felt that officers often felt that the role of community provisions conflicted with and was often seen as not being compatible, even not complementary to services provided by the local council.
(Focus group 12)

Conversely, where Black groups tried to initiate partnerships, it seemed an uphill struggle to convince people to come on board. Some felt this was because of racism and a feeling of not being connected to the issues, or that the issues were too 'hot' for their committees (e.g. Black women's group supporting refugees).

The respondents said that new requirements were constantly evolving and they needed help to engage in seeking or maintaining strategic partnerships:

In one borough many of the BME organisations are new as there are not many established BME groups left in the borough since the cuts began in the early 90s. The groups questioned felt that these groups do not have the experience to be able to develop effective capacity building to develop strategic partnerships and, therefore, would need support in this area.
(Focus group 11)

This is similar to Black housing associations. These have not been long in the field and have not yet had the opportunity to build up capital reserves and infrastructures that allow them to deal with all the new regulations and the competitive nature of the market on an even footing to longer established associations.

Moreover, the lack of strategic partnership between the council and the voluntary sector can be seen in the cases where the council is now providing a service that the groups themselves used to provide at a cheaper cost. However, this does not include the unique added value and culturally sensitive services that Black and Minority Ethnic groups are able to provide (focus group 1).

The case studies (particularly case study 2 in Box 10 in the section on 'Accountability' later in this chapter) illustrate that, sometimes, the expertise and potential of a group are not recognised.

Box 7   Case study 1

The Peepul Centre would house a healthy living suite, a childcare centre, training facilities, restaurants, business development units and a conference centre. It was also keen to develop platforms for arts and sports development. It sought strategic partners for all of these areas.

It was largely down to the vision and belief of key individuals that partners came on board, for example Leicester College and De Montfort University for education and training, the Leicestershire Health Authority for the healthy living centre and accountants KPMG put in a great deal of voluntary time in helping to develop the business plan.

For other areas, some consultants initially worked on the basis that they would not get paid unless the funding came through. They did this partly believing in the concept but also wanting to be part of something that was going to be a model of public private and voluntary sector partnership.

Help needed

Too many of the groups we contacted did not know who they could ask for advice on funding and relied on staff or management committee contacts. One faith group in Greenwich reported, 'We get by with God's help'.

In many cases, groups were appreciative of the local authority's help where officers had tried to be supportive, but the groups were not always 'in the know' about funders.

Some suggested they would like assistance from experienced fund-raisers and experts, but from an approved list. This could be tiered into those who come with track records, references and successful outcomes and those who are newer on the circuit but with good credentials (see section earlier in this chapter on 'Use of fund-raisers'). This list could be developed and maintained by a Black-led national organisation or the National Council for Voluntary Organisations (NCVO) with a steering group that has good representation from the Black Voluntary and Community Sector.

They also wanted to see better co-ordination between funders, to enable logical application forms and consistent processes, with clear criteria.

Respondents also felt the need for web sites and directories of funders with timescales, application forms and other information available online. Although this information is available, the fact that the groups did not seem aware of it reflects our belief that many groups need to have 'capacity building' to use such resources in terms of both IT and making sense of the content.

Box 8   Case study 1

Sport England and the Arts Council had African or Asian workers who had been tasked with encouraging applications from minority ethnic groups. These officers were hugely supportive and facilitated what were in the end successful applications.

Sport England (East Midlands) was particularly keen to look at ways in which sport could assist capacity building and social inclusion, and it was this recognition of seeing sport not just as sport but rather as a vehicle

(continued)

---

for much greater agendas that was liberating for all concerned. The Arts Council had a Black woman as a lead assessor who was rigorous in her approach but also understood the issues well. She was able to cut through what otherwise had been painstaking explanations of the way in which communities were organised.

Accountability

The levels of scrutiny levelled at the Black Voluntary and Community Sector were thought to be at best sporadic and at worst discriminatory. The first step towards fairness in accountability was to have clarity regarding the criteria for application, which were then followed through to the objectives of the grant bid. It is these that a project should be assessed against.

Criteria

As political agendas change, so too do criteria for funding. Currently, it is abundantly clear that 'social inclusion' and 'community cohesion' are the buzz words. Anything to do with crime prevention and resistance to drugs and substance misuse is similarly weighted. Several funders list ethnic minorities, disabled people and women as priorities, but then have little knowledge of these areas themselves. Many funders were vague about the criteria. Their learning curves about the new agendas were often limited by their lack of critical analysis of the 'new' concepts.

Groups reported difficulties in keeping up with the changing agendas and the need for them to be just as acquainted with the jargon as full-time professionals in funding organisations.

Even where applications had been canvassed, the refusal seemed to be based on something that the groups had not been aware of in the first place.

Groups were asked about what they thought were important criteria for funding the Black Voluntary and Community Sector. They put forward a number of diverse opinions, ranging from merely filling gaps in existing provision to fulfilling a wider role, empowering the community.

They suggested the criteria were to:

- fill gaps in service provision (groups were divided on this – some felt that the voluntary sector should not be doing things that the local authority should be doing, especially if there were no resources from them)

- assist in self-help and community development

- encourage regeneration and neighbourhood renewal

- make up for past discrimination

- help empower communities.

Instruments

While funders were of course interested in content, many also placed a heavy emphasis on the group's ability to produce documentation and management frameworks. Most groups reported that the basic items they supplied were annual accounts and annual reports. Depending on amounts and/or funders, they would also supply: business plans; strategic plans; annual projected outcomes; quarterly or half-yearly reports; employment monitoring; service-level agreements; output numbers (including numbers of service users broken down by each event or activity); monthly cash flows; minutes of meetings, etc. (focus group 2).

Very few had business plans in place. There were a few exceptions – mainly among the larger funded groups. The best example was Operation Black Vote, which has a ten-year plan. Three of the groups questioned had a strategic development plan:

The BME organisations lucky enough to receive funding from the local authority complained of the mountain of quarterly and monitoring statistics they have to compile, often different methods of providing information to similar council departments.
(Focus group 2)

One group expressed the view that local authorities in particular had got so embroiled in the performance indicator culture that it was the creation of the template rather than its contents that seemed to excite them.

In accounting for funds, there were the perennial difficulties of the amount of work involved in maintaining financial records together with – for newer groups especially – the lack of basic knowledge of financial systems and management. Added to this was the workload of payroll. Very often, groups just paid accountants to do all of this for them.

In developing the capacity of the Black Voluntary and Community Sector, this is, we feel, one area that needs attention. Groups themselves need to have a basic understanding of these issues so they can at least check the work of whoever does it for them. This could be a second-tier organisation, like The 1990 Trust, which is currently developing plans to help here.

Conversely, one group told us of their accounting being smarter than the local authority's. When doing yearly returns, the group showed actual expenditure but invoiced only for the grant that was awarded, sending a covering letter explaining all of this and showing the reality and where they had had to find other funds. This also illustrated the leverage that the council money offered. However, the officer could not cope with this and said the actual spend had to equal exactly the grant figure. This did not seem to make any sense but in the end the group had to comply just to get the grant.

Evaluation

All groups accepted the need for accountability but many complained that it seemed to be a one-way street, in that the voluntary sector was always being evaluated – but how did the group evaluate the authority?

This could be crucial for partnerships, particularly when it came to deciding on funding next time (see case study 2 in Box 10 below). Many expressed the view that the difference in requirements was enormous and, for a small group on small amounts of money, the paperwork required was over-burdensome. This was ironic given that many public authorities found it so hard to supply the information we needed on funding to the sector, broken down by ethnicity.

All groups felt that they could really use some assistance in getting together business and strategic plans, and in how to draw annual operational objectives from these.

Groups most likely to succeed were those who could tabulate, cross-reference and cite targets, key measurements and completion dates. This needed to be followed by a tracking system across the indicators and scales to measure achievement. The problem is that the people very good at doing these things are not necessarily able to deliver. They are just very good at making it look as though they have done so.

Box 9   Case study 1

One funder insisted that the way we would be assessed would be by question and answer correspondence and refused to do it by meeting. This resulted in at least three rounds of separate long lists of question to which we responded, only to be met with more questions, some new, some based on our answers. This could have gone on for ever had we not insisted that we meet with the chief executive.

This comment is taken from a recent statement from the Peepul Centre.

(continued)

Current policy implementation has one simple flaw – there's a tendency to repeat the failures of the past by forcing new ideas through the same old delivery mill. The infrastructures and mechanisms used to facilitate the policy become the assassins of its real intent. Accountability gone mad drives an overburdening interpretation of policy as it cascades down through the tangled mass of middleman-bureaucracy; the emerging programmes often bear no resemblance to the original ideas. The policy-makers don't get what they want and the communities on the ground lose out. Worse still, the process itself consumes a greedy chunk of the resources simply to show that the system is working.

Every tick, check and audit conducted in a culture of 'can't do, can't trust' deprives the people most in need from the thing they most want. The funding torrent quickly becomes a trickle on the ground, while huge coffers are locked behind impenetrable red tape. A relentless need to measure, monitor and justify is strangling the life out of that most delicate of social nuances – selfless social endeavour.

Sometimes the most valuable outputs cannot be easily measured. Try measuring the feel-good factor, sense of collective responsibility, democratic empowerment and the fostering of a 'can do' culture. Nobody would dispute that these attributes should lead to better communities. Yet they are often tossed aside in pursuit of the next checklist of hard facts.

We need unhindered, less bureaucratic mechanisms to get the resources directly to people who need them through community-based mechanisms. A confident society is one that believes in and trusts its communities to deliver.
(Words highlighted by the Peepul Centre)

Box 10 Case study 2

A key funder wrote to us refusing our grant application but in the process was almost slanderous in implications that our business plan wasn't transparent. We complained and made it clear that we would not accept this kind of comment. Suddenly there was a huge turn around and we eventually got the funding. Too much of the funding process depends on the quality of personnel and the politics. The stated criteria hardly seem to matter.

When it came to the end of year 1, we had been working with what we thought was a partnership with other agencies in the area. However, the local authority came and evaluated our project – we had to fill in evaluation forms and have a scrutiny meeting with three officers. We were given a glowing report. However, we could not evaluate them. This was particularly unfair as the local authority then had the power to decide where its allocation of money for this particular issue would be used and in this process they allocated most of it to themselves! Besides the unfair nature of the accountability process it also highlighted the fact that the council did not see the working with the voluntary sector as an investment which needed to be sustained. This was also hard to accept because it was apparent that we had succeeded in reaching young people and working with them on this issue that the council had never been able to do.

The group had frustrations concerning the constant turnover in council staff and the ever-changing council policies. They also felt that some of the requirements were unfair. In the early days, the council always wanted a place on the management committee and to attend every management meeting. The group argued that this changed the whole dynamic whether they were White or Black because of the power relationship. In addition, they did not see why they should have voting rights but not bear the

(continued)

same responsibility as other management committee members. This was eventually changed after many years of argument, so that the officers would come to meetings once a quarter and would always check to see if that meeting would be appropriate for them to attend.

The group were also concerned that the council held copies of all their minutes because the group felt these were confidential and wanted assurances that the council would keep them locked up.

Service-level agreements also seemed confusing and unfair. Confusing because the officers did not seem clear whether the agreement meant that the council would not compete by providing similar services or whether the targets set would be used against the group. If the group failed to get 25 users, for example, for a particular project, would the funding be cut? The group felt that the same level of toughness was not applied to the local authority, which for many years had failed to provide appropriate services for Black communities.

Nowadays, it was more a case of groaning every time new personnel came to them as a project officer. Their different ideas, coupled with lack of experience, were very frustrating, as the groups had to keep explaining themselves. The groups were experienced and proficient in accounting for the grant monies but new officers often did not have financial expertise or experience of the relevant communities and therefore the group spent ages just explaining the systems and issues. Still, more often than not, the officers tried to exert monitoring functions from a position of assumed superiority. Some of the councils' systems seemed archaic and nonsensical but the group had to work to those.

Issues of inequality

Most of the individual groups questioned thought that discrimination does play a role in terms of access to funding and the types of organisation likely to be supported.

It was even suggested that, where members of a community were in prominent positions politically, the projects were more likely to be supported by the local authority. Moreover, it was stated that Black and Minority Ethnic organisations that have political support were not 'targeted in the same way' in terms of performance.

All but one of the groups questioned said they knew of other BME organisations that have experienced discrimination in terms of funding.

Greenwich groups felt there was less likelihood of African and Caribbean groups getting funding, as opposed to all other equalities groups.

Quoted in an article in *The Guardian*, Mike Eastwood, Director of the Directory of Social Change, highlighted some of the dangers of hidden inequalities in the funding process:

> I think there's a rather circular argument along the lines of 'there's no racism in the voluntary sector because the voluntary sector is not racist'. Because these organisations are more involved at the cutting edge of minority issues, there's a sense that they are less likely to be institutionally racist – which, of course, is not necessarily the case.
> (Snell, 2000)

However, perpetuating disadvantage through inaction is every bit as dangerous as conscious discrimination. Institutional racism can be described as a 'range of long-established systems, practices and procedures, which have the effect, if not the intention of depriving ethnic minority groups of equality of opportunity and access to resources' (Lattimer with Trail, 1990, p. 56).

The political nature of obtaining funding

Groups in Leicester and London felt that several local councillors had a vested interest in some groups and, even though they did not sit on committees, could still control who got what and where.

There was also an anomaly in some areas where it was a stipulation of funding that a council representative attend all management committee meetings. However, they could not be subject to the legal requirements of the other members of the management group. Many felt this was an affront to self-organisation and displayed a lack of trust. It was accepted that there should be regular meetings with the council representatives and accounts could be held, but keeping minutes of meetings was too controlling.

However, the contrary view was also expressed that some link officers were too remote and hardly seemed interested at all. Some felt this seeming disparity exemplified the politics involved where groups were seen to be a challenge politically.

The move to unitary status for Leicester City Council in 1997 meant that some groups that were previously funded by the County Council would now be funded by the City Council and that had led to a discrepancy in salary grades and staff conditions. They also felt that there was now money given for inflationary rises or pay rises and therefore the group struggled to find the extra cash or money for stakeholder pension schemes.

In one London borough, it was reported that things have changed for the worse since the BME development team had been disbanded. Many of the groups felt that there was not a clear-cut strategy for developing or supporting BME voluntary organisations in the borough.

This illustrates how important it is for groups to feel they have a good link into the local authority for some clear advice. Many felt that the move away from equality units in local authorities has not been beneficial to the development of Black Voluntary and Community Sector groups.

Several groups were wary of being dependent on government funding but felt that the options were closing down:

> To find favour you have to be uncontroversial. Black grass-roots politics does not find favour in many places despite good work.
> (Focus group 3)

Charles Secrett from Friends of the Earth questions the validity of the voluntary sector working in partnership with the government. He claims:

> The point of the sector is to be independent and there is a danger of watchdogs becoming lapdogs when in partnership with the government.
> (Quoted in Hill, 2000)

Additionally, there was a perception that local authorities (i.e. the main funders of the Black Voluntary Sector) were non-committal and fickle about the needs of the Black Voluntary Sector and more inclined to the politics of the 'Third Way'. The result of such ideological forces at work was that current funding policies and arrangements did not reflect the stated needs and principles of the BME sector.

Political environments also affected cuts in funding and groups were very aware of the 'flavour of the month' syndrome.

Funding discrepancies

Several groups complained that the voluntary sector always seems to be disproportionately affected when local authorities make cuts. Although many groups in the voluntary sector are similarly affected, they felt it particularly hit small voluntary organisations, which included many Black groups. What seems like a fair cut policy across the board disproportionately affects these projects, and in particular Black groups, because they are smaller projects. For example, a larger organisation could probably cope with a 10 per cent cut in funding, but, for smaller organisations, it could be the difference between surviving or not:

One of the policies the borough has perused to bridge the gaps between their income and expenditure has been a wholesale disposal of council-owned properties to the private sector. Given its proximity to the city, certain properties are highly sought after by estate agents and affluent individuals.
(Focus group 2)

Another focus group were critical of the council's moving away from supporting voluntary organisations by offering cheap rents for use of council-owned premises. Increases have gone from a few pounds to £5,000 in one year, with some organisations even being asked for backdated payments of five years. This has put many groups in an impossible position (focus group 1).

Many felt that massive changes in grant-aid personnel at short notice meant ineffective hand-over information between council officers.

Council staff, in particular BME staff, are often scared to stick their necks out in supporting the voluntary sector against the background cuts in staffing and changes in employment conditions. Many operate in an atmosphere of fear. Groups maintained there are few BME people in position of power to support BME projects.
(Focus Group 3)

The state lead on funding, of whichever party, always seems to waiver between assimilation and integration, crime reduction and youth containment.
(Focus Group 16)

Box 11 Case study 1

While we were an Asian women's group in a small terraced house and accepted what the officers had to say, we were no problem. However, once we found our voice and were able to influence voting intentions, we became a threat. Even worse, when we looked as though we were about to pull off one of the biggest projects Leicester had ever seen and we

(continued)

had some economic muscle with key business people, there were serious attempts to kill the project. Now things have come full circle with new leadership of the council shrewd enough to know it's better in the long run for everyone to work with us and share the vision and be a part of the credit.

Box 12 Case study 1

Most of the discrimination is not overt but sometimes it gets pretty close. Some of it was down to a lack of cultural understanding, like an assessor who wouldn't believe that Asian weddings drew more than a couple of hundred people. So we've invited him to one so he can see for himself, if he can get in the door!

Some funding agencies found it difficult to accept that although it is an Asian women's group it would also be open to everyone and will actively encourage that.

We want to be leaders in the whole field not just in cultural enclaves.

The group also told of their experience of the least discrimination coming from business people. It was money that spoke and therefore they would do business on the group's terms.

Box 13 Case study 2

We were asked about what guarantees we could offer for the proper financial management as another African Caribbean group in our area had fallen down on this.

We felt that because of the 'sins' of one Black group others were unduly scrutinised as if we are all the same. So many White groups must also falter but are others compared to them? It would have been fine if the question had stopped at quality assurance and around proper systems, that we understand, but to

(continued)

put it into the framework the question of another African group highlighted their propensity to stereotype and not see distinctions between one Black group and another.

Civic engagement, capacity building and social inclusion

Questions were asked about how people grew from being involved in their organisation and whether they knew of people who went on to do other things.

Respondents reported a range of reasons why people got involved. Some did so because of deeply held convictions and a commitment to act; but most became aware when an issue personally affected them or their family. The role of community workers and youth workers was crucial here, as they could often alert individuals to issues in a proactive way and help them see what was on offer. As one community worker put it:

Increasing awareness of themselves and their environment helps them to be active in that world, rather than just passive recipients of it.

Communication

The groups used various methods to encourage participation. These included:

- newsletter

- word of mouth

- large inclusive meetings

- community meetings

- group's own publicity about campaigns

- deliberate capacity-building programmes

- headhunting/talent spotting

- cultural education/music

- mentoring, which is seen as a major method for getting more BME people involved in BVCS projects, activities and local issues.

Of those involved in the groups, everyone was pleased to have become involved in the Black Voluntary and Community Sector. However, for some, especially full-time workers, they felt it had tended to take over their lives and many sacrifices had had to be made. Some expressed this as part of the journey in anti-racism – a path which they felt was never easy.

A Black Women's group in Tower Hamlets, for example, said:

The majority of people from the refugee community came into the UK due to civil war in their country. Their qualifications are not recognised and as such they are unable to find jobs in their own areas of expertise, i.e. doctors working as cleaners, porters, waiters. Prominent men and women are now doing menial jobs to survive. Getting involved in the BVCS can raise self-esteem, let you know you are not alone and help others back into the mainstream of society, a positive influence on life chances.

All the organisations questioned were able to provide examples of people who have developed their interest inside and outside the sector, such as becoming schoolteachers, social workers and working in other professional occupations. In addition, gaining experience as management committee members was seen as a very important springboard for encouraging community participation. However, it was pointed out that these individuals need to be strong, confident and determined in order to deal with expected rejection and the lack of respect that BME groups face on a daily basis from 'other professionals in the field' (focus group 14).

Members of the groups reported that members they knew of were:

- involved in police consultative committees, crime and disorder committees and racial harassment panels

- school governors

- magistrates

- involved in other management committees

- involved in mental health organisations

- involved in drama groups

- involved in refugee groups

- one woman in a women's organisation had started by taking her child to playgroup, then, with encouragement, had become a playgroup management member while training in childcare; later she went on to become a local councillor.

Some groups spoke of their purposeful activities to encourage political and social enfranchisement. For example, Operation Black Vote in London actively works on challenging the democratic deficit in Black communities. Its MP shadowing scheme has been a resounding success, with 700 applications for 20 shadowing places offered by MPs.

Civic engagement has long been a stated aim of the BVCS in more or less overt ways. This challenges the notion that Black communities do not wish to be involved or are apathetic. On the whole, they want to be involved, but cannot always find the doors to open up that involvement. Here the BVCS is crucial:

The recent changes to policies re funding have only exasperated social exclusion. Some argue that institutional racism has been taking place against certain BME voluntary organisations, as seen by the decreasing level of support to BME groups, which has been falling disproportionately to other groups in the borough. In fact, in the mid-80s the council total capital and revenue funding to the voluntary sector was nearly 13 million per year. Much of it was targeted to BME groups.
(Focus group 13)

The same group also expressed the view that people who are disaffected by poverty or discrimination may tend to 'drop out' and that they tried to support people and encourage them to be socially included by making them welcome at all times. They provided platforms for them to speak and helped them to assess available services.

In addition, for some members of BME groups, there was neither a commitment to social inclusion, nor acceptance of the important role that BME organisations can play in tackling social problems.

Box 14 Case study 1

What is now the Peepul Centre began as Belgrave Girls' Youth Movement and among its very first activities were women-only swimming, badminton, developing a newsletter, sewing classes, camping trips and other outings. Through women organising together we gained confidence in what could be achieved. We set up an employment project which offered training in key skills and worked almost in an advocacy role to match women to their goals.

Many women came to us through our domestic violence work and were often so despondent it took several months of support and hand-holding to get them to a point of believing that they could even attempt to get a job. Giving them an application form and an advert in the beginning would have sent them running for cover. We were able to provide for these women and many others a holistic approach to getting them where they wanted to be. Childcare, housing, benefits, health issues all had to be sorted out. Another important aspect was to teach them about their rights. And it worked. So many of the women who have come through our doors have now gone on to have solid employment or have developed their own businesses, or have become involved in public life that we have lost count. The investment is huge but so is the pay-off and it is hard to think of other agencies that can provide the same level of care and support.

(continued)

Capacity building should be recognised as crucial to the real support of the Black voluntary sector. Funders, particularly those providing public sector support, have exhaustive requirements and assessment procedures. To date, in our case, the risk in developing the project financially is heavily lain on the community organisation submitting the request, with limited resources provided to enable the requirements to be met. This is a severe disadvantage to organisations seeking support, particularly to Black organisations like ourselves which originate from and represent inner city disadvantaged and socially excluded communities. We have persevered due to our belief that, unless we have the courage to take the risk and continue, nothing will change.

Box 15 Case study 2

The group organise specific capacity-building programmes, and were doing so before the term was coined. Then, they called them self- or personal development or empowerment courses. The courses offered a combination of Black history, self-esteem, knowledge of the systems and structures in Britain, and were peppered with practical tasks. These included shadowing a key local figure for a day, or finding out about the way in which the police service were organised and then reporting back to the group.

The group had found that many people on the course had been inspired and had their eyes opened beyond their immediate locality. They were much more confident and had more aspirations than before. However, what was sometimes depressing, as one of the workers put it, was that the operation of choice to realise the aspirations was often bounded by economic reality. Hence, to move house or to change schools was often not possible.

Benefits of a strong Black Voluntary and Community Sector

Participants were clear that there were enormous benefits in Black-led separate provision. These included being able to claim rights and, as a group, to organise and be involved in a way which individuals, who could often be subject to the winds of racism, might find difficult.

Among the benefits they quoted were:

- empathy and understanding – no stereotypical barriers

- understanding of cultures, which reduces isolation and language barriers, and thus enables effective communication

- a safe environment for development and opportunities that would not otherwise exist – partly because of racism

- a stronger voice in policy development

- strengthened relationships with other agencies, consultation, development, capacity building, etc.

- a unique understanding of what is required – they understand and believe in their community, they allow Black groups to have the cultural space to articulate their needs.

The existence of the Black Voluntary and Community Sector was seen as being vital for ensuring self-determination and local empowerment. All the participants questioned saw social inclusion as the major added value provided by these groups over other local providers questioned:

All those questioned stated that a strong umbrella body is needed to help support and develop BME voluntary groups. It was also felt that BME people were not properly represented within the sector and that BME groups are normally at the bottom when it comes to access to funding – despite the fact they make up most of those with identified problems.

However, BME people need to take control of their own destiny and not be the subject of control by others.
(Focus group 16)

The only disadvantages that groups could think of were rooted in the misunderstandings of funders about the purposes and intentions of Black-led groups and in the competitive nature of funding, which sometimes caused jealousies and infighting. However, the latter was something that was seen to be a feature across the voluntary sector as a whole.

In an ideal world

At the end of the sessions, groups were asked what they would see as an ideal situation for the development of the Black Voluntary and Community Sector, besides limitless pots of money.

What the groups wanted for themselves

The groups wanted adequate and continuous funding for three to five years, which would provide the necessary stability and resources for sustainable development. It would also allow a planned financial and fund-raising strategy.

They would also welcome the development of a shared asset base for groups or consortia of groups, which would help with the sometimes extortionate rent and rates that groups had to pay. It would also foster sharing of expertise and resources, and be a wiser investment for funders. The groups also felt they needed dedicated funding workers to help the sector. They also wanted to be able to share more good ideas and opinions.

They felt they needed to be well funded and recognised for their efforts by local and national authorities.

What the groups wanted from funders

The groups suggested more grant-giving bodies should consider core funding for longer and that the government should recognise that a strong and empowered Black Voluntary and Community Sector benefits all communities rather than just fulfilling a service provision role.

They called for transparency in the funding processes and sought a practical model of how funding policy actually translates from the top to the ground.

The groups believed funders needed to look at how to simplify and better support community regeneration policies and programmes on the ground in a real sense.

They also felt there was a need to pilot best practice regarding the way the government liaises with the voluntary sector and the Black community in particular. The funders needed to have a model in order to encourage holistic and seamless provision of services.

Funders should get away from throwing money at problems and look more carefully and thoughtfully at how the sector could overcome problems on the ground through true partnership.

The groups believed that, by streamlining systems, the government could convert money spent on bureaucracy (on both sides) into money used for services of benefit to people in the inner city.

They felt the government should look at the real value of social capital – in other words, the importance of social networks in developing personal relationships that underpin a rich community.

The groups thought there should be new thinking on how community-led regeneration should be enabled and supported – not hindered and drowned through fear and ignorance on the part of the funding bodies.

They also argued there needed to be a change to a 'can do' mentality in the management of funding, from a 'can't do'/'more than my job's worth' attitude.

4 Results from questionnaires to public authorities and funders

Survey response

The response rate from funders to the questionnaires was quite low with 30 returns, equivalent to 20 per cent. Other researchers have also experienced problems getting a high-level return on mail questionnaires. For example, McLeod *et al.* (2001, p. 14) achieved about a 20 per cent return rate on their postal survey to Black and Minority Ethnic Organisations, which they noted 'is about the average for a postal survey of this type'. This is probably due to several factors, as we note below, but the general conclusion we arrived at was that this method does not work very well for the constituencies we are addressing.

As a consequence, it is important to note that our analysis of the returns does not draw broad or general conclusions. However, our discussion here is more like viewing a number of case studies, which each provide a valuable insight.

Although a large number of institutions and organisations expressed a desire to complete and return the questionnaire to the Trust, for a wide range of reasons they could not. Among the reasons given for not returning the questionnaire were the following.

- The institution did not have sufficient staff available to complete the form in a timely manner.

- The institution did not collect data or information in a form that would be useful to the research project.

- The individual(s) who could provide the information could not make this research a priority.

- The data being asked for was divided among several units or divisions, and it was not possible to collect and collate it in a timely manner.

- The institution did not find this type of research useful or productive, and perhaps it even perpetuated the problem.

Public sector bodies, perhaps out of a sense of legal responsibility, were more likely to respond or provide detailed reasons why they could not complete the questionnaire than private sector institutions, which were under no direct obligation to co-operate with researchers. Although all the organisations and institutions acknowledged the need for transparency, this notion was interpreted very differently. For some, it meant supplying information to virtually anyone that asked. For others, it meant accountability and access to only their constituents or more immediate authority.

There were some complaints about the questionnaire, even among those who did return it. Some felt that it was too long – 15 pages – and that perhaps that would deter many from completing it. For smaller institutions with limited staff, the survey demanded a significant amount of time and energy, which some felt could be put to better use. Others felt that there were some terms on the form that they did not understand or could easily define, e.g. 'civic engagement'.

Overwhelmingly, however, most of those who returned the questionnaire were able to respond to all the questions, and even to give a great deal of additional data and supplementary documents. Many felt that the process of gathering the data and information, and reflecting on the probing questions being asked, was extremely helpful to their work. In a few instances, the questions on the survey generated productive staff or team meetings where, for the first time, the meaning of funding or relating to the Black Voluntary and Community Sector was discussed. All of those surveyed, including those who did not return the questionnaire, expressed a strong interest in seeing the results of the study.

The funding issues raised in the questionnaire occur in a very dynamic external atmosphere for the sector, their funders and other stakeholders. The Race Relations (Amendment) Act (2000), Human Rights Act (1998) and other legal changes that have happened or that are going to happen must be understood and appreciated by funders in order to fully appreciate their impact on civic participation by Black and Minority Ethnic communities.

These changes include incorporating new European directives on employment and race into domestic law (under Article 13 of the Amsterdam Treaty, 1997). The Employment Directive will, for the first time, provide protective legislation in employment for sexual orientation, age and religion or belief, and the Race Directive will necessitate changes to the existing Race Relations Acts.

There are new obligations for the public sector around the General Duty and Specific Duties in the Race Relations (Amendment) Act (2000), which will mean higher scrutiny regarding employment and the delivery of goods and services. For example, the majority of public authorities will have to assess, consult on and monitor their policies for their impact on so-called 'racial' groups. In addition, if they employ over 150 people, they will need to monitor staff by racial or ethnic group. This includes not only applicants for posts, but also staff in post, staff who are subject to grievances or disciplinary hearings, who applies for and who receives training, the results of appraisals and performance assessment, and staff who leave. All of the results of monitoring and assessment must be published annually.

These changes will also affect many in the private and voluntary sector, because public authorities must ensure that any procurement arrangements are compatible with meeting the general and specific duties under the Act. It should therefore follow that there will be an effect on funding priorities.

Nonetheless, we feel that voluntary organisations which seek funding to address incidents of racial violence and harassment may still struggle to receive financial support because of the disproportionate involvement of Black people in the criminal justice system and their lack of political representation in the UK policy-making bodies. This is because the government emphasis for funding is on service delivery.

It is in this context that the Black Voluntary and Community Sector must operate and attempt to meet its objectives of delivering equality. Only a few respondents mentioned any of these issues, although there was opportunity to do so, based on the wording of the questions.

Question 2, for example, which asked how recipients understood or viewed the importance of the sector, was answered in generic and general terms by nearly all.

Organisational details

This section of the questionnaire sought to solicit basic information not only about the institutions and organisations that received the survey, but also about the general demographic atmosphere in which the groups work.

The groups were from three different geographical categories: local, regional and national. The groups can also be divided according to the different constituencies with which they were trying to work. While some institutions targeted the Black Voluntary and Community Sector more generally, others focused on particular strands within Black and Minority Ethnic communities – such as elderly people or those needing health services. This meant that groups were addressing very different communities. The constituencies were further varied by factors such as age, gender, or specific sub-groups of Black and Minority Ethnic communities.

The survey asked groups not only to identify the proportion of Black and Minority Ethnic individuals in their constituency, but also to supply data on the gender and disability populations under their remit. While a few were able to provide or obtain this latter data, most did not.

This suggested to us that further work might be required to examine whether the issue of multiple or cross-cutting discrimination (e.g. the situation confronted by a disabled Asian woman) is addressed programmatically or thematically by many funders. However, most borough authorities, though not all, were better able to provide these data. This is probably due to the remit and sensitivity that the boroughs must have in order to do their work effectively.

A few of the institutions in our survey did take a more comprehensive approach. The Age Concern London group, for instance, were able to provide not only race, gender and disability data, but also data by age, and the specific details on the interrelationships between these different categories.

It is also unclear in much of these data whether refugees and asylum seekers are included. Only the Bexley, Bromley and Greenwich Health Authority indicated that its numbers did not include either refugees or travellers.

Involvement with Black communities

We asked a wide range of questions about involvement with Black communities, for example the following.

- Please explain how you consult with voluntary and community organisations and if possible give examples. (If you have any consultation guidelines please could you attach them.)

- Do you have any particular ways of ensuring consultation with Black communities?

- How do you ensure that Black communities are involved in developing and implementing policy and in the strategic planning processes in your organisation?

Essentially, the goal was to determine how funders relate to Black Voluntary and Community Sector groups and the larger Black and Minority Ethnic community. We also explored issues of perspective and accountability. Respondents were given the opportunity to discuss not only their successes and best practices, but also the difficulties they face in attempting to reach out to and work with the Black Voluntary and Community Sector.

Funders and other stakeholders were consciously involved with the Black Voluntary and Community Sector in many ways. These included:

- consultations

- media outreach

- strategic planning and partnerships

- building consortiums or other special groups

- surveys

- site visits

- attendance at meetings

- conferences, training sessions and seminars

- focus groups

- non-financial support.

For several stakeholders (e.g. East Midlands Regional Assembly, Haringey Council, Lambeth, Southwark and Lewisham Health Authority), the most important outcome of these varied approaches was that they changed their policies after these engagements, in an effort to be more responsive to the needs of the sector. These respondents stated that these interactions and critical feedback from the sector had an impact on, and changed, their strategies and views.

For example, the Equality Action Plan developed by the Community Fund was driven in part by the consultation process. In a similar way, Haringey Council's Race Equality Joint Consultation Committee grew out of the consultative engagements between the sector and the council. Among a number of funders, more strategic and service-specific plans are now in place as a result of feedback from the sector.

For the sector itself, the willingness of stakeholders to adjust their practices as a consequence of work with groups representing Black and Minority Ethnic communities validates their purpose and reasons for being.

Interestingly, only two public sector groups, Southwark Council and the London Fire and Emergency Planning Authority, mentioned the role of the Black Voluntary and Community Sector in the development of their Race Equality Scheme. Under the Race Relations Amendment Act (2000), many public bodies are required to develop race equality schemes that follow very strict guidelines. These plans should be developed in direct consultation with the communities most affected by them. It is likely that many of the public authorities have not completed their race equality schemes, though they are obligated to do so.

Any omission of the Black Voluntary and Community Sector as a consulting partner in the development of the race equality schemes would be a double irony. First, the schemes are aimed at delivering equality to Black communities, how would this be known? Second, the legislation itself explicitly says that public bodies should set out how they plan to consult Black and Minority Ethnic communities and their representatives about the public body's plans.

Some respondents sought to be systematic and even philosophical in their efforts to reach out to the voluntary sector. The Lambeth, Southwark and Lewisham Health Authority uses what it terms a 'community development' approach in its work. Under this plan, funding is seen in a holistic manner, in other words that it has as much to do with community development, empowerment and capacity building as it does with the specific issues being addressed by the submitted proposal. Some funders referred to this idea as a 'community strategy'. This perspective means that Black and Minority Ethnic issues are embedded in the funding strategy from the beginning. In this particular London borough, they are aiming to link funding and work with the Black Voluntary Community Sector to the council's existing structures and funding initiatives.

Consultations

Many of the respondents stated that they invested heavily in consultation with the Black Voluntary and Community Sector, and recognised the importance of taking an aggressive posture towards this issue. These consultations included formal and informal, highly structured and loosely structured, ongoing and periodic. Most respondents were very involved in consultation in a number of ways. Many stated that 'consultations have caused policy changes' in how they go about their work.

Several respondents who answered this query – the Bexley, Bromley and Greenwich Health Authority, Commission for Racial Equality, Allen Lane Foundation and City Parochial Foundation and Trust for London (CPFTL) – stated that they did not have any specific consulting work or programmes with Black Voluntary and Community Sector groups. They noted that Black and Minority Ethnic communities were part of the general outreach that was done.

CPFTL did state, however, that it does individual work with voluntary sector groups, including the Black Voluntary and Community Sector, on organisation development issues. Although the Commission for Racial Equality does not do any direct consulting at the grass-roots level, it works through the Race Equality Councils, which do.

Media outreach

Information-sharing through media outreach – publicity about the organisation and the grants available – was important to all the respondents.

In general, publicity about the grants available sought to emphasise the needs and priorities of Black and Minority Ethnic communities. The way in which this was done, however, was very uneven. While some funders were clearly knowledgeable about a variety of avenues to reach Black and Minority Ethnic communities (minority ethnic press, local radio), others did not mention these at all. Funders and other stakeholders used radio and print advertisements to reach the voluntary sector.

The institutions and organisations surveyed were concerned about the use of language in their outreach efforts. Some felt it needed to be plain (Charities Aid Foundation), in a variety of tongues other than English (Haringey Council) and even that the format was appropriate (i.e. that application forms be provided in large print for elderly people or those with visual limitations). All of the groups used the Internet, employing both email and web sites as forms of providing and receiving communications from the voluntary sector. The organisations provided funding information, press releases and even funding applications on their websites.

None of the respondents mentioned the effectiveness of email and Internet communication as a means of reaching Black and Minority Ethnic communities and the Black Voluntary and Community Sector in particular. Some respondents (Community Fund) were more aware than others of the need to use Black media outlets as a means of reaching the sector. This included advertisements in Black newspapers as well as using Black radio stations. Respondents found that, through these means, they could more directly inform Black and Minority Ethnic communities about funding opportunities and how to access them. In particular, they found Black talk radio was an excellent means by which to make contact with,

and get feedback from, Black communities.

Some groups published the list of Black Voluntary and Community Sector organisations they funded. This was to let Black communities know that it was not just predominantly White-led organisations receiving funding and in order to refute a popularly held view among Black organisations that funding goes only to predominantly White-led organisations.

Strategic planning and partnerships

In addition to consultations, respondents involved the Black Voluntary and Community Sector in more organic ways.

Many respondents used local strategic plans (e.g. Central Learning and Skills Council, Hackney Borough Council, Leicestershire Learning and Skills Council) as a means of involving Black and Minority Ethnic communities. The plans, of course, were developed by public sector institutions that were trying to address very broad agendas and constituencies.

Many stakeholders who wanted direct contact with the BVCS used other strategic partnerships outside of these plans (e.g. East London and the City Health Action Zone, the Commission for Racial Equality, Lambeth, Southwark and Lewisham Health Authority, Leicestershire Constabulary, London Fire and Emergency Planning Authority, Southwark Borough, Tower Hamlets Borough).

Partnerships seem to be the preferred way of involving Black Community and Voluntary Sector groups for both private and public sector funders. Indeed, this is likely to be the prime route of engagement of the future.

The Commission for Racial Equality (CRE), for instance, has decided to completely restructure its relationship with the Race Equality Councils (Commission for Racial Equality, 2002).

The Race Equality Councils are presently funded under Section 44 of the Race Relations Act 1976. Under new so-called 'modernisation' guidelines, the Commission predicts that a progressive transformation will occur, as more efficient Race Equality Councils adopt the partnership model and survive, while those who resist will likely fall away. It is starting to transfer, in large part, the funding of the Race Equality Councils from the Commission to the private sector. The Councils have previously served as the Commission's link to the Black communities and the voluntary sector.

Building consortia or other special groups

Apart from the more economically driven partnerships, some respondents noted that they took the lead in, or helped to build, multi-ethnic consortium projects (e.g. Age Concern London) that were both short- and long-range in their outlook.

Funders have also created special groups that are formally concerned with racism and equality. These groups offer a great deal of potential for helping in race equality service delivery. The Leicestershire Learning and Skills Council, for example, helped to organise the Equality Taskforce. Leicestershire Constabulary put together the Racist Incident Review Panel. Haringey Council created the Race Equality Joint Consulting Committee.

These kinds of initiatives demonstrate the seriousness on the part of some funders to go beyond merely funding Black Voluntary and Community Sector groups. They show a willingness to establish projects and units that will deliver equality. It is unclear how the funders directly affect the ability of groups from this sector to obtain funding. However, it was encouraging that they appeared to recognise the importance of the work of the Black Voluntary and Community Sector, and the need to be facilitators, rather than to be bureaucratic or create political obstacles.

Surveys

Telephone and postal surveys were also employed by at least one respondent (Community Fund) to find out how much was known about their organisation.

However, this strategy seems to be the least used among funders and others, and was perhaps the least effective. The Community Fund gave no details regarding the nature of the surveys, conclusions drawn, or the response rate. These are highly costly endeavours, which we believe are likely to yield very few cost-effective results.

Before dismissing this approach, though, as marginally useful at best and a waste of time and money at worst, we feel it would perhaps be useful to engage with professional pollsters who are more familiar with conducting surveys. From our experience of surveys for projects and in our own networks, we have found that telephone surveys are often the easiest and quickest way of engaging people. If the right questions are asked in the right way, very productive insights may be gained. In fact, in our experience, a common complaint from Black and Minority Ethnic communities is that their opinions and views are rarely, if ever, solicited.

Site visits

Two respondents (Community Fund and the East London and the City Health Action Zone) stated that their staff paid visits to applicants from Black and Minority Ethnic communities as a way of ensuring that the highest possible quality could be achieved in getting a response from Black communities. This means of interacting and connecting with Black Voluntary and Community Sector groups registered highly with the communities. It gave funders a close insight into the work and environment of the people they were funding. It also gave the groups an opportunity to demonstrate what they had done, their staff, the people they worked with and the community.

Since so few respondents mentioned that they visited groups in this way, it is possible that they do not have the resources or staffing to do so. However, given the valuable results of this type of outreach, we believe it would perhaps be wise to determine how, if even in a limited way, some form of site visit could occur.

Attendance at meetings

Some groups (e.g. East Midlands Regional Assembly and Leicestershire Learning and Skills Council) attended meetings and other events held by Black Voluntary and Community Sector groups and in the Black and Minority Ethnic communities as a whole. Several of the institutions and organisations surveyed stated that they not only attended events in these communities, but also conducted strenuous evaluations afterwards of their participation, the success of the event and other relevant details. These events were viewed by both funders and the Black Voluntary and Community Sector groups as pivotal to understanding (and responding to) the issues faced by these communities.

Conferences, training sessions, seminars and focus groups

Hackney, Haringey and Southwark Borough Councils all held conferences, seminars, training sessions and even focus groups targeted specifically at the Black Voluntary and Community Sector. Haringey Council was the only respondent that stated that it used focus groups as part of its work with the voluntary sector.

These efforts were geared towards raising the profile of the funding organisation in Black communities and also creating direct links and networks with them. In the end, it meant that it was easier for institutions to distribute materials and information in places where they had built ties, and for the Black communities to submit well-prepared applications and to get funding.

Non-financial support

Those surveyed were also questioned regarding the support they gave to the Black Voluntary and Community Sector that was not directly financial in nature, or had little to do with the application for funding process. This question was raised to find out how comprehensive the methodology that was used by funders in the work with the sector was.

Among the services and other assistance given were:

- interpretation and translation services
- technical assistance
- staff training
- capacity building
- free training around tax effectiveness
- access to research information
- pro-bono consultancy
- management and development training
- application surgeries
- presentations
- community liaisons
- participation in community events.

From the Black and Minority Ethnic communities' perspective, the purpose of these efforts was to keep Black communities and their issues high on the agenda of funders and other stakeholders.

Difficulties in consultation

Respondents noted important difficulties in their attempts to better serve or reach the Black Voluntary and Community Sector. These views tended to divide into two different categories: problems or issues that were rooted in the funding community; and problems or issues that were linked to sector or Black and Minority Ethnic communities. Only a few of the respondents saw past a 'blame us – blame them' attitude and argued that perhaps there were concerns on both sides that had to be addressed.

In the first category (problems within the funding community), one issue that was raised by some respondents was their perception that Black Voluntary and Community Sector groups did not view the funding organisation as relevant to their issues. Age Concern London, for example, felt that they were seen as a predominantly White-led organisation.

Others felt that the funding community has not addressed consultation issues with the Black Voluntary and Community Sector in a strategic way. While they felt consultation was important, very few indicated that they approached it systematically, consistently or within a framework that was comprehensive and visionary. Some funders noted that the limited funding available to, and received by, Black Voluntary and Community Sector groups affected that sector's ability to have effective engagement with public bodies. In a self-critical way, a few respondents admitted that they were not reaching some Black and Minority Ethnic communities or small Black Voluntary and Community Sector groups. As a result, they claimed that they have struggled to fund the sector, despite it being a priority.

The danger of over-consultation was also mentioned. This seems to refer to the process of too much talking and too little action. Conversely, others said that feedback to applicants was missing, therefore compounding the problem. Underscoring these deficiencies is the fact that complaint mechanisms and other forms of structured accountability would appear not to exist. It was in this context that respondents admitted the need for culturally appropriate services.

A number of points were raised regarding what respondents perceived to be the cultural, political and structural problems internal to the sector. Some of these took the form of 'blame the victim'. One funder stated that language (in total, 193 languages were spoken by their various constituents) and cultural issues formed a barrier to outreach and effective communications between the overwhelmingly White funding community and Black and Minority Ethnic communities. More than one respondent cited divisiveness and rivalries in these communities as an issue of major concern.

They contended that, unless the funding community understood how these conflicts function, it was very difficult to know what relationships were going to cause problems.

Structurally, Black Voluntary and Community Sector groups lack management and organisational infrastructure, according to several respondents. These inadequacies help to foster and perpetuate the lack of relationship that groups in the sector have with statutory agencies and funders. As a result, they had few 'champions' pleading their case before these bodies and institutions on a consistent basis. As one said, Black and Minority Ethnic groups are not 'keyed into the process of involvement and consultation'. Few argued with this contention.

Civic engagement – participation in the democratic process

As recent studies have demonstrated, civic engagement by Black and Minority Ethnic communities is in desperate need of a boost (see Ali and O'Cinneide, 2002). From low voter turnout, to the absence or low representation of Blacks and Asians in the nation's political institutions, the promise of democratic participation seems a long way off. It is widely accepted within the Black community that the sector is vital in bringing Black and Minority Ethnic representatives into mainstream political life. Although many groups within this sector are engaged in service delivery, these activities are often seen from the perspective of civic engagement. Some Black and Minority Ethnic groups are explicitly involved in civic issues.

It is important that funders recognise the relationship between the Black Voluntary and Community Sector and civic participation. Most of the current Black (elected and appointed) government officials, at both local and national level, initially came out of this sector and view it as an indispensable catalyst enabling them to obtain political office.

In discussing the importance and need for Black and Minority Ethnic communities to be more involved in civic engagement, many respondents used similar terms. They spoke of the Black Voluntary and Community Sector in terms of: 'enabling' (London Ambulance Service); 'more involvement' (Leicestershire Constabulary); and 'greater participation' (Age Concern London, East Midlands Regional Assembly and Haringey Council). They all felt that it was imperative to be active around and in the decision-making processes that shape Black and Minority Ethnic community life. There were two respondents (Allen Lane Foundation and Community Fund) who said they were unfamiliar with the term 'civic engagement', although this may reflect more the views of the individuals completing the questionnaire than of the institution.

In many ways, however, the terms used by respondents still assume a more passive and, ultimately, consultative role for groups in the sector and for the communities as a whole. Only two respondents used the arguably stronger and more democratic term 'empowerment' (City Parochial Foundation and Trust for London). The Commission for Racial Equality argued strongly for 'ownership of one's community' as a criterion for civic engagement. These remarks were in recognition that genuine democratic involvement meant that Black communities did not just inform decision making, but also had a seat at the decision-making table. We believe that this level of advanced thinking should be the objective of the BVCS, funders and other stakeholders alike.

It was not clear whether most respondents saw the relationship between funding levels for the sector and the extent of civic engagement. No respondent made this link in their explanation of the term 'civic engagement'. It is also notable that no one addressed the issue of political under-representation faced by Black and Minority Ethnic communities.

The recognition, however, that decision making regarding Black community issues should be democratic is a positive sign. This 'lack of

meaningful dialogue', as the Central Learning and Skills Council put it, is, we feel, politically debilitating and needs to be urgently addressed.

Social inclusion – 'everyone has opportunity'
While civic engagement addresses concerns regarding political power and the ability to influence or determine public policy, social inclusion looks at the broader landscape of equality, quality of life and opportunity. Social data consistently demonstrate that Black and Minority Ethnic communities are disproportionately dispossessed and at the bottom of most social indices, including the areas of employment, education, housing, health care and in the criminal justice system (see Box 1 in Chapter 1).

Most respondents seemed to recognise the importance of resolving these issues and the critical role the sector has in constructing solutions to problems experienced by Black and Minority Ethnic communities. Respondents discussed the need to: fight 'exclusion' (Allen Lane Foundation); provide 'opportunities' (Central Learning and Skills Council and Newham Borough); and 'include everyone' (Charities Aid Foundation, East London and the City Health Action Zone, East Midlands Regional Assembly).

As Haringey Council declared, it is time that previously excluded groups be given an 'equal voice'. Respondents argued the need to go beyond simple tolerance and advocated the progressive stance of 'valuing difference' (Leicestershire Constabulary).

Several respondents (Age Concern London, Commission for Racial Equality, Lambeth, Southwark and Lewisham Health Authority) linked social inclusion to the political and legal rights afforded to Black and Minority Ethnic individuals. Ultimately, social inclusion will mean that these rights are respected, defended and perhaps expanded as the situation demands. New laws and policies from the Council of Europe and European Union (European Directives under

Article 13 of the Amsterdam Treaty 1997) focus on the rights of racial minorities and others that have faced discrimination. This will push this discussion forward.

Capacity building – enabling those marginalised to participate in civic engagement

Both Black Voluntary and Community Sector groups and funders agreed that lack of capacity was a major factor preventing or perverting the ability of the sector to engage in civic participation and respond to social inequalities. As the London Ambulance Service remarked, these are 'investments that facilitate social inclusion'. Yet the two different sides' understanding of what is meant by capacity building can differ significantly. While some stakeholders view any interaction with sector groups as 'capacity building', the groups themselves define the term in very concrete and material terms as merely having sufficient resources. The groups view access and ownership of resources as a starting point for development and sustainability.

Age Concern London offered an extremely useful and straightforward definition of capacity as: 'having the skills and resources to meet objectives'. This interpretation keeps the focus appropriately on Black Voluntary and Community Sector groups achieving their primary goals and not just on capacity building for its own sake.

Along these lines, we believe it is essential that funders recognise and address the issue most critical to the sector: namely, sustainability. Only the Commission for Racial Equality and Newham Borough Council identified this as being central to the success of the sector. It appears that few funders and other stakeholders want to resolve this central issue facing the groups in this sector, in an era where funding is harder to come by and existing funding is being curtailed or eliminated altogether.

Many respondents (Charities Aid Foundation, City Parochial Foundation and Trust for London, Community Fund, Haringey Council,

Leicestershire Learning and Skills Council and Leicestershire Constabulary) noted an array of specific non-monetary concerns regarding capacity building. This included tasks such as:

- training
- strategy planning
- project management
- team building
- infrastructure building
- organisational development
- general management
- legal skills
- constitution development
- payroll management
- financial management
- publicity
- networking
- building a database
- building a library
- administration self-management.

Funding information

Historically, from the mid-1970s to the present, funding of the Black Voluntary and Community Sector has come primarily from the public sector. As McLeod *et al.* (2001) noted, nearly two-thirds of the funding received by Black and Minority Ethnic organisations in 1998–99 came from central government, local authorities, grants from other statutory bodies, or contracts with statutory bodies (see Figure 2).

Data from these researchers indicated that very little funding actually went to these groups from trusts and foundations, and that remained constant

45

Figure 2 Distribution of funds to Black and Minority Ethnic organisations, 1998–99

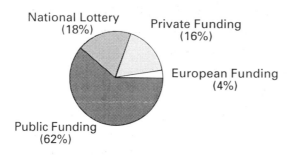

National Lottery (18%)
Private Funding (16%)
European Funding (4%)
Public Funding (62%)

Source: McLeod *et al.*, 2001, pp. 36–8.

over an extended period. For instance, they concluded that only 1.4 per cent of trust funding went to Black Voluntary and Community Sector groups in 1990. By 1999, nearly a decade later, the figure had risen to only 3 per cent (McLeod *et al.*, 2001, p. 6)

The trusts gave not only a fairly low percentage of funding to the sector but also relatively small amounts. According to McLeod *et al.*'s (2001) study, although there were a few large grants, most grants tended to be approximately for only £5,000. Furthermore, they generally came from a tiny circle of funders and were overwhelmingly concentrated in London.

One of the most significant findings of that research was that 'more than 80 per cent of funders in the 1990 study believed that ethnic minority status should be disregarded when considering applications' (McLeod *et al.*, 2001, p. 6).

When the Single Regeneration Budget Challenge Fund came into operation in April 1994, it merged 20 funding programmes, then worth £1.4 billion. Three of these programmes had previously been earmarked for projects aimed specifically at minority ethnic groups (Section 11, Ethnic Minority Grants and Ethnic Minority Business Initiative) with funding that had amounted to a total of £66 million pounds (Hansard 321.3.94, Col. 918). Once these funds were included into the Single Regeneration Budget, these resources were available to any project that was/is consistent with the broader aims of the Budget.

In 1997, the Local Government Information Unit reached the conclusion that, while urban policy initiatives were indirectly connected to meeting the needs of the minority ethnic groups, they have never explicitly targeted racial disadvantage. Therefore, any progress made in terms of addressing racial disadvantage was seen to be incidental rather than intrinsic to the policies dictated by the Single Regeneration Budget.

Representation

For the groups surveyed, Black and Minority Ethnic representation on both boards and staff was generally below their percentage in the national population (7.1 per cent) and significantly below the London (27 per cent) and Leicester (45 per cent) rates. This occurred disproportionately across the spectrum from the very small staff size (1.5 at the Allen Lane Foundation) to the larger staff (2,067 staff officers and 950 support staff at the Leicestershire Police service). Although they were not specifically asked, none of the respondents offered an explanation of why the proportion of Black and Minority Ethnic staff was so low, or how it might impact on their work with those communities and the Black Voluntary and Community Sector. Nor did they say what they were going to do about the situation.

It is similar with board memberships. Many groups in the survey had only one or two – or even no – Black and Minority Ethnic representation. The boroughs, in the main, seemed to do much better. Newham had 23 such representatives out of 60 elected members. In Haringey, 22 per cent of the council members were from these communities. Tower Hamlets, which has a large proportion of Black and Minority Ethnic residents, had 22 Black members out of a council of 50.

Essentially, the public sector is doing much better on representation than independent charities.

This is likely to be because the public bodies are more accountable to their citizens and obliged by statute to reach out to the Black and Minority Ethnic sector.

On account of the lack of data, it is not possible to correlate Black and Minority Ethnic representation on the staff and boards of the funding organisations with the rate, type and amount of funding that the sector receives. It is clear, though, that the lack of representation on the various charities boards and staff means that a Black and Minority Ethnic perspective is missing at a crucial stage in the decision-making process regarding funding. In most instances, staff within funding organisations played an important role. They were involved in determining who to reach out to, how that outreach was conducted, how to respond to interested parties, how applications were handled, the decisions on funding, the follow-up to those who were and were not funded, and in monitoring of the funding that did occur. In all these circumstances, the experiences and sensitivities of the staff and / or board members who are making decisions play an important role.

comes from trusts or charities. Of those trusts and charities that responded to our survey, there were suggestions that many were targeting the Black Voluntary and Community Sector. We were, however, unable to find evidence to support this from the data received from these organisations.

The views from the groups about the difficulties in obtaining funding were due in part to structural barriers and in part to lack of cultural understanding or racism. For example, structural barriers included: the capacity of groups to complete complex application forms, which differed from funder to funder; the ability to keep up to date with ever-moving programmes, guidelines and jargon; the ability to complete business plans and other types of performance indicator planning documents. This was compounded by the fact that, unlike public sector organisations and other funding bodies, the majority of groups in the Black Voluntary and Community Sector were not able to buy in expertise, nor did they have the infrastructure of a wide pool of employees allowing them to train people.

We were impressed with some trusts that were considering funding second-tier Black Voluntary and Community Sector organisations that would be set up to help smaller groups with their management and systems and planning processes.

The importance of second-tier organisations was also reflected in the need to have 'cushion' organisations for funding. These can help with up-front funding until grant money is received and with payroll systems, accounting systems, etc.

Recommendation

We believe that there is a crucial need for a site or institution to provide free or low-cost capacity-building training to the sector. This issue was raised repeatedly in the focus groups. While many funders noted that capacity building was a problem, none advanced any concrete ideas about

how to address the problem. A collaborative effort to establish such a centre would go a long way in addressing a concern expressed by all stakeholders. In addition, such a centre would be able to provide central services such as payroll and templates for minutes, strategic and business plans, and a range of managerial and administrative support services.

Funding is only short-term

The other common complaint from groups was around the short-term nature of funding and the fact that it was still not recognised that funding was needed for core costs as well as project costs. There are ways in which, in applying for project costs, core costs can be built in – for example, an organisation needs to raise a percentage of core costs for administrative support, copying, travel, phones and rent every time a project is submitted. In this way, core costs need not seem to be bald requests for money. However, many groups need assistance with this kind of approach and second-tier organisations that aim to support the development of smaller organisations by helping them with their infrastructure (e.g. financial management and administration) may well be able to help.

We were aware that some trusts (not specifically included in this research) were moving towards a principled stand of consideration of three to five-year funding for all voluntary organisations and to providing funding for core costs. However, this was less likely to be the case with public sector organisations. This was possibly because they are more focused on outcomes of a piece of work than on general principles of supporting the sustainability of the sector. However, this was not a universal conclusion.

We felt there was a tension between what is mistakenly seen as 'professionalism' – highly structured, meticulously planned and evaluated projects – and dealing with the more necessarily relaxed management style and operations of grass-roots work. This tension was exacerbated by expectations from local authorities that the Black Voluntary and Community Sector can respond with speed and in recognisable formats with the acceptable phrases and jargon to consultation calls, application procedures, etc.

This expectation is totally disproportionate to the pace at which the voluntary sector can also adapt, understand or deal with the new funding regimes – or even its desire to do so. The 'contract culture' has meant the sector, despite being on the front line in the fight against poverty and exclusion, is at risk of being overlooked by the very programmes that are supposed to address these issues.

Recommendation

The use of a second-tier organisation that had expertise in this area could help alleviate some of these problems.

Funders were trying to engage more with the Black Voluntary and Community Sector

Public and private sector bodies were increasingly using a wider range of methods to contact and engage with the Black Voluntary and Community Sector and those that did this encouragingly reported that, as a result, many policy strands were amended.

With the implementation of the Race Relations Amendment Act (2000), many public authorities will have a specific duty to consult, particularly on any new policies that may have an adverse impact on any racial group. Potentially, this gives a great opportunity for groups from the sector to comment on funding strategies and requirements. However, it is too early to assess whether optimum use will be made of these procedures.

Recommendation

In our view, work needs to be done to build the knowledge base of communities to understand the requirements of the Race Relations Amendment Act (2000) and other relevant legislation, such as the Human Rights Act (1998), so they know what they should expect and how they might respond. In parallel, many public authorities, from our experience, are also unclear of the duties on them or what to do with the results of such consultation. While the specific duties of the Act do not apply to private or voluntary sector bodies, it would be beneficial for them to adopt and adapt to their circumstances the principles behind the requirements.

Some Black Voluntary and Community Sector groups are overused

Several groups reported a growing fatigue with the constant requests for consultation and partnership approaches, which were often perceived to be one-sided. Many felt obliged to respond to requests, but did not feel that they could expect the same feeling of obligation from authorities to requests from the Black Voluntary and Community Sector for partnership or information. Where partnerships were operational, many groups felt that there had been a lack of clarity from the start about the balance of power within the partnership – that is, the levels of participation, control of agendas and decision-making powers were not equitable.

Recommendation

In our view, it is imperative that, where partnerships are invoked, the early stages must include agreement on the respective expectations and obligations, and on the level of power that each party has. Where a local authority partners a Black Voluntary and Community Sector group, resources and procedures for decisions are not matched. This can lead to ill-feeling that partnership is no more than a tokenistic link used to gain central government funding for the authority, with little return to the group itself.

There is a need to bridge the gap in understanding

Overall, it is apparent from the research that the perceptions from funders and from the sector about funding, and in particular its relationship to capacity building, civic engagement and social inclusion, are not the same. The findings indicate that there is much work to do.

Recommendation

In our view, funders must be encouraged to keep adequate, accessible and transparent data. It is nearly impossible to rectify the situation, in order to improve the effectiveness of the sector, without this information.

We also believe all those involved will need to develop long-term strategies and vision for the development of the sector. With sustained development and ample investment – capacity building – and by working in clear and equitable partnerships, we believe the Black Voluntary and Community Sector is the best vehicle for guaranteeing the social inclusion and civic engagement of Black communities.

Notes

An Introduction to The 1990 Trust

1   We use Black throughout this bid as its inclusive political meaning to cover Asian, African and Caribbean individuals and groups.

Chapter 1

1   Funding for empowerment and self-organisation has always been more problematic. The conceptual models for funding race issues in Britain have, at their worst, operated on a colour-blind model, then on an improved multi-cultural model and, at best, anti-racist models (Chauhan, 1990).

2   In fact, there has been a history of Black people organising as far back as the reign of Elizabeth I in England. She was the first monarch to order the deportation of Blacks and was seminal to the development of slavery.

3   'Sou sou' (Trinidadian), 'Pardner' (Jamaican) or Asian mortgage clubs (Sivanandan, 1982).

4   BBC News World Edition, http://news.bbc.co.uk/2/hi/uk_news/england/1357865.stm.

5   The 1990 Trust has written a separate paper on 'Managing Diversity' as a concept. It is available from The 1990 Trust.

6   The 1990 Trust is currently running three civic-engagement programmes with women's groups in Lambeth, Hillingdon and Bedford with assistance from the Adult Community Learning Fund.

Chapter 2

1   London: Greenwich, Hackney, Haringey, Hillingdon, Lambeth, Lewisham, Southwark, Tower Hamlets. Leicester: Beaumont Leys, Belgrave, Braunstone, Highfields, Narborough Road, Humberstone.

References

Ali, R. and O'Cinneide, C. (2002) *Our House: Race and Representation in British Politics*. London: Institute for Public Policy Research

Arnstein, S. (1969) 'A ladder of citizen participation', *Journal of the American Institute of Planners*, Vol. 35, No. 4, pp. 216–24

Audit Commission (2002) *Comprehensive Performance Assessment*. London: Audit Commission

Bowling, B. (2000) *Violent Racism – Victimisation, Policing and Social Context*. Oxford: Oxford University Press

Brisia, K.A. (1966) *Urban Churches in Britain, a Question of Relevance*. World Studies of Churches in Mission Series. London: Lutterworth Press

Chauhan, V. (1990) *Beyond Steel Bands and Samosas*. Leicester: National Youth Bureau

Chouhan, K. and Jasper, L. (2000) *A Culture of Denial – The 1990 Trust Report on the Racist Murder of Stephen Lawrence*. London: The 1990 Trust

Chouhan, K. and Jasper, L. (2000b) *Milton Keynes Youth Service – Racism and Racial Attacks*. London: The 1990 Trust and REDRAP Partnership

Commission for Racial Equality (CRE) (2002) *Getting Results: A New Approach to Funding Local Racial Equality Work*. London: CRE

Daily Mail (1978) cited in Chouhan, K. and Jasper, L. (2001) *A Culture of Denial*. London: The 1990 Trust, p. 37

Davis, S. and Cooke, V. (2002) *Why Do Black Women Organise: A Comparative Analysis of Black Women's Voluntary Sector Organisations in Britain and Their Relationship to the State*. London: Policy Studies Institute for the Joseph Rowntree Foundation

Department for Education and Science (DfES) (2002) *Statistics of Education: Permanent Exclusions from Maintained Schools in England*. London: DfES

Department for Education and Science (DfES) (2003) *Aiming High: Raising the Achievement of Minority Ethnic Pupils*. London: DfES

Dobson, J. (2000) 'Neighbourhood strategy raises hopes', *The Guardian*, 9 November

European Monitoring Centre (2002) 'Summary Report on Islamophobia in the EU after 11 September 2001'. Vienna: EUMC, www.eumc.eu.int

Gray, J. (2002) 'The reckoning', *New Statesman*, 30 September, p. 22

Hill, N. (2000) 'Partners or puppets?', *The Guardian*

HM Treasury (2002) *The Role of the Voluntary and Community Sector in Service Delivery: A Cross Cutting Review*. London: HM Treasury

HM Treasury (2003) *futurebuilders*. London: HM Treasury

Home Office (1998a) *Compact on Relations between Government and the Voluntary and Community Sector*. London: Home Office

Home Office (1998b) Active Community Unit Code of Good Practice: www.homeoffice.gov.uk/racecom/active

Home Office (2000) *Race Equality in Public Services*. London: Home Office

Home Office (2001) *Community Cohesion: A Report of the Independent Review Team* (the Cantle Report). London: Home Office

Home Office (2002) *Black and Minority Ethnic Voluntary and Community Organisations: A Code of Good Practice*. London: Home Office

Joseph Rowntree Foundation (1997) *Urban Regeneration and Ethnic Minority Groups: Training and Support in City Challenge Areas. Findings* No. 227. York: Joseph Rowntree Foundation

Lattimer, M. with research by Trail, P. (1990) *Funding Black Groups: A Report into the Charitable Funding of Ethnic Minority Organisations*. London: Directory of Social Change in association with the Urban Trust

Lemos, G. (2000) *Racial Harassment Action on the Ground*. London: Lemos&Crane

Local Government Information Unit (1998) *Race and Regeneration: A Review of the Single Regeneration Budget Challenge Fund*. London: Local Government Information Unit

McLeod, M. (1996) *Managing Change: The Black Voluntary Sector in the West Midlands*. Warwick: University of Warwick

McLeod, M., Owen, D. and Khamis, C. (2001) 'Black and Minority Ethnic Voluntary and Community Organisations: Their Role and Future Development in England and Wales. London: Policy Studies Institute for the Joseph Rowntree Foundation

National Council for Voluntary Youth Services (2002) *The Role of the Voluntary Sector in Public Service Delivery; a Cross Cutting Review*. London: NCVYS, www.ncvys.org.uk

Nationality and Immigration Act (2002) *Secure Borders, Safe Haven: Integration with Diversity in Modern Britain*. London: The Stationery Office

Office of the Deputy Prime Minister 'Delivering thriving, inclusive and sustainable communities in all regions', http://www.urban.odpm.gov.uk/programmes/srb/

O'Rawe, M. (1997) *Human Rights on Duty*. Belfast: Committee on the Administration of Justice (CAJ)

Ouseley, Sir H. (2001) *Community Pride, Not Prejudice. Making Diversity Work in Bradford*. Bradford: Bradford Vision Partnership, www.bradford2020.com/pride/report

Owen, D., Green, A., Pitcher, J. and Maguire, M. (2002) *Minority Ethnic Participation and Achievements in Education, Training and the Labour Market*. Warwick: Centre for Research in Ethnic Relations and Institute for Employment Research at the University of Warwick

Performance and Innovation Unit, Cabinet Office (2001) *Improving Labour Market Achievements for Ethnic Minorities in British Society*. London: Performance and Innovation Unit, Cabinet Office

Phillips, M. (1993) 'Anti-racist zealots drive away recruits', *The Observer*, 1 August

Runnymede Trust (1997) *Islamophobia: A Challenge for Us All*. London: Runnymede Trust

Sivanandan, A. (1982) *A Different Hunger: Writings on Black Resistance*. London: Institute of Race Relations

Snell, J. (2000) 'An equal struggle?', *The Guardian*, 5 April

Social Exclusion Unit (2000a) *Minority Ethnic Issues in Social Exclusion and Neighbourhood Renewal*. London: Social Exclusion Unit

Social Exclusion Unit (2000b) *A Strategic Framework for Neighbourhood Renewal*. London: Social Exclusion Unit

Stephen Lawrence Inquiry (1999) *Report of an Inquiry by Sir William Macpherson of Cluny*. London: The Stationery Office, CM 4262-I

Tomlins, Professor R. (2003) 'Bedfordshire Black and Minority Ethnic Accommodation Needs Study', commissioned by Bedfordshire Consortium of Housing Associations. London: The 1990 Trust and De Montford University, Leicester

Ward, L. (2002) 'Black vote remains elusive'. *The Guardian*, 15 October

Williams, Z. (2002) 'Life's a Lotto', *The Guardian*, 15 October

Appendix 1

Groups that returned the questionnaire

1   Age Concern London

2   Allen Lane Foundation

3   Baring Foundation

4   Bexley, Bromley and Greenwich Health Authority

5   Central Learning and Skills Council

6   Charities Aid Foundation

7   City Parochial Foundation and Trust for London

8   Commission for Racial Equality

9   Community Fund

10 Diana, Princess of Wales Memorial Fund

11 East London and the City Health Action Zone

12 East Midlands Arts

13 East Midlands Regional Assembly

14 Government Office East Midlands

15 Hackney Borough Council

16 Haringey Borough Council

17 Joseph Rowntree Charitable Trust

18 Lambeth, Southwark and Lewisham Health Authority

19 Leicester Social Services

20 Leicester Education Department

21 Leicestershire Learning and Skills Council

22 Leicestershire Police

23 London Fire and Emergency Planning Authority

24 Lloyds TSB Foundation

25 London Ambulance Service

26 Newham Borough Council

27 Southwark Borough Council

28 Tower Hamlets Borough Council

29 Tudor Trust

30 Voice East Midlands

Appendix 2

Groups that returned the questionnaire – by sector

Foundations

- Allen Lane Foundation
- Baring Foundation
- Charities Aid Foundation
- City Parochial Foundation and Trust for London
- Community Fund
- Diana, Princess of Wales Memorial Fund
- Joseph Rowntree Charitable Trust
- Lloyds TSB Foundation
- Tudor Trust

Council authorities

- Hackney Borough
- Haringey Borough
- Newham Borough
- Southwark Borough
- Tower Hamlets Borough
- Leicester Social Services
- Leicester Education Department

Civic authorities

- Bexley, Bromley and Greenwich Health Authority
- Government Office East Midlands
- East London and the City Health Action Zone
- East Midlands Regional Assembly
- Lambeth, Southwark, and Lewisham Health Authority
- Leicestershire Police
- London Fire and Emergency Planning Authority
- London Ambulance Service

Other groups

- Age Concern London
- Central Learning and Skills Council
- Commission for Racial Equality
- Leicestershire Learning and Skills Council
- East Midlands Arts
- Voice East Midlands

Appendix 3

Selective list of groups participating in focus groups or individual interviews

Please note that this list represents only those groups happy to be named. There were ten additional groups not included on this list.

Leicester

1 Beaumont Leys Community Forum

2 Bliss

3 Chaos

4 Mowmacre Play Association

5 Next Steps

6 Belgrave Association

7 Savera

8 Shree Sanatan Community Association

9 Belgrave Mela

10 Shree Prajapati Community

11 Belgrave Baheno – The Peepul Centre

12 Bhagini Centre

13 East West Community Project

14 Jalaram Temple

15 Islamic Mosque

16 Braunstone Volunteers

17 Braunstone Community Association

18 Braunstone Residents' Association

19 Braunstone Motor Project

20 Highfields Play Association

21 Each one teach one

22 Mandata Community Association

23 Council for Youth

London

1 Cypriot Elderly and Disabled Group

2 Turkish Cypriot Women's project

3 The Council of Asian People

4 African Caribbean Leadership Council

5 Hillingdon Somali Women's Group

6 Hillingdon Traveller Support

7 Hillingdon Asian Women's Group

8 Hillingdon Chinese School

9 Somali Advice Centre – Hayes

10 Grange Park Hindi Society

11 African Caribbean Society

12 Hindu Society

13 African Caribbean/West Indian Society

14 Confederation of Indian Organisations (UK)

15 African Foundation for Development (AFFORD)

16 West Indian Standing Conferences

17 Organisation of Blind African Caribbeans

18 Afro-Asian Advisory Service

19 Black Women's Health and Family Support

20 Operation Black Vote

21 National Assembly Against Racism

22 Black Londoners' Forum

23 Lambeth Independent Advisory Group

24 Single Parent Aid